It Feels Like I Was Already Here

Sergio Gomez Solo Exhibition

GOSS183 Publishing House | Bloomington, Illinois

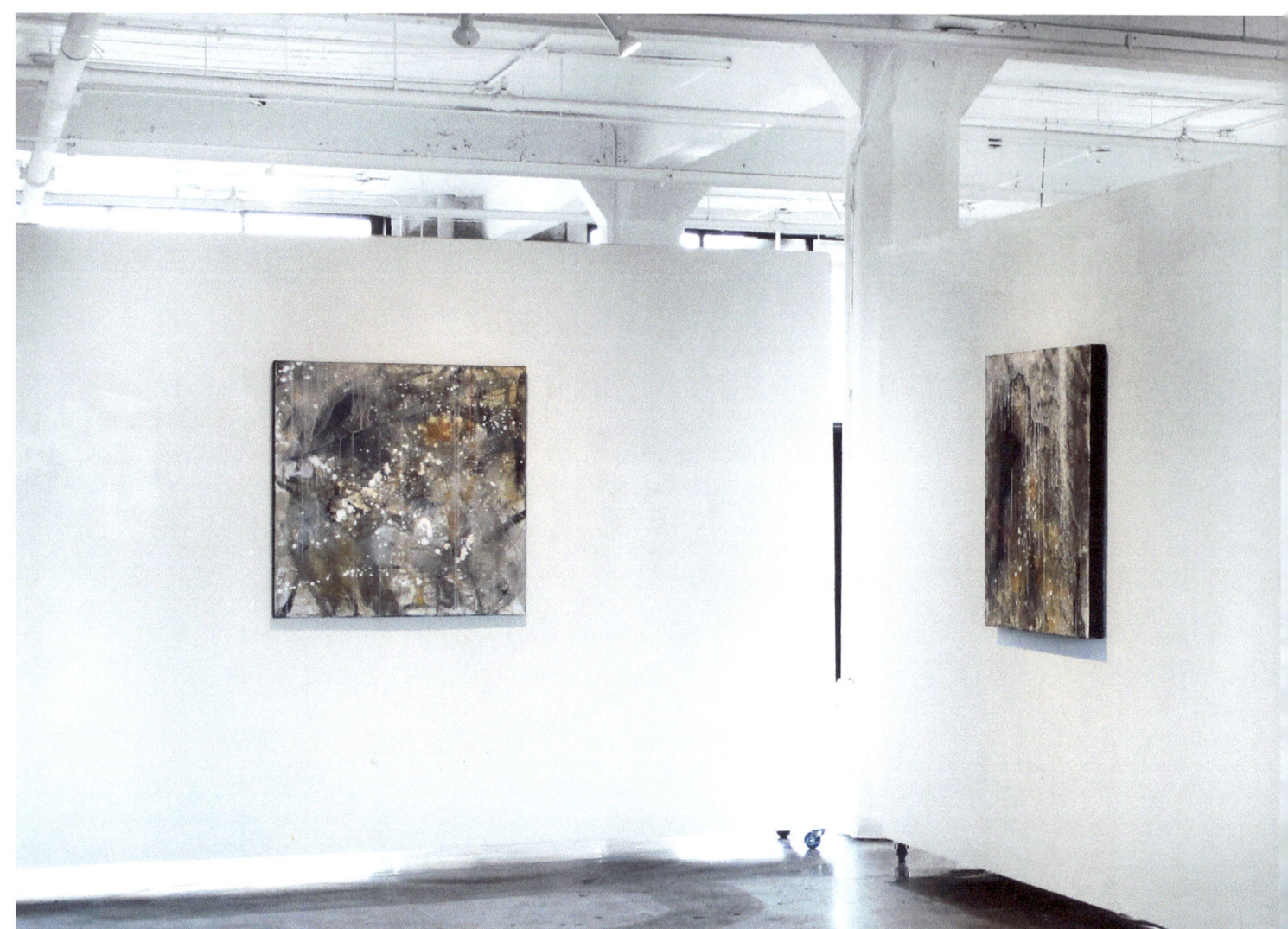

The Art of
Sergio Gomez

"In Gomez' paintings, the door is suggested merely by its absence. The figure inhabits our world and, standing at this doorway, is implicitly about to become a part of it. Gomez' world is communitarian and engaged; the openness and action of the viewer is assumed just by the act of gazing at the painting. We have stopped at an open door, and we are now in relationship with the ones on the other side."

"If at its best art is an invitation to relationship, the works of Sergio Gomez are bold and complex provocations to a series of interconnected meetings. Gomez' use of the human figure grounds his work in the depth of human concerns;

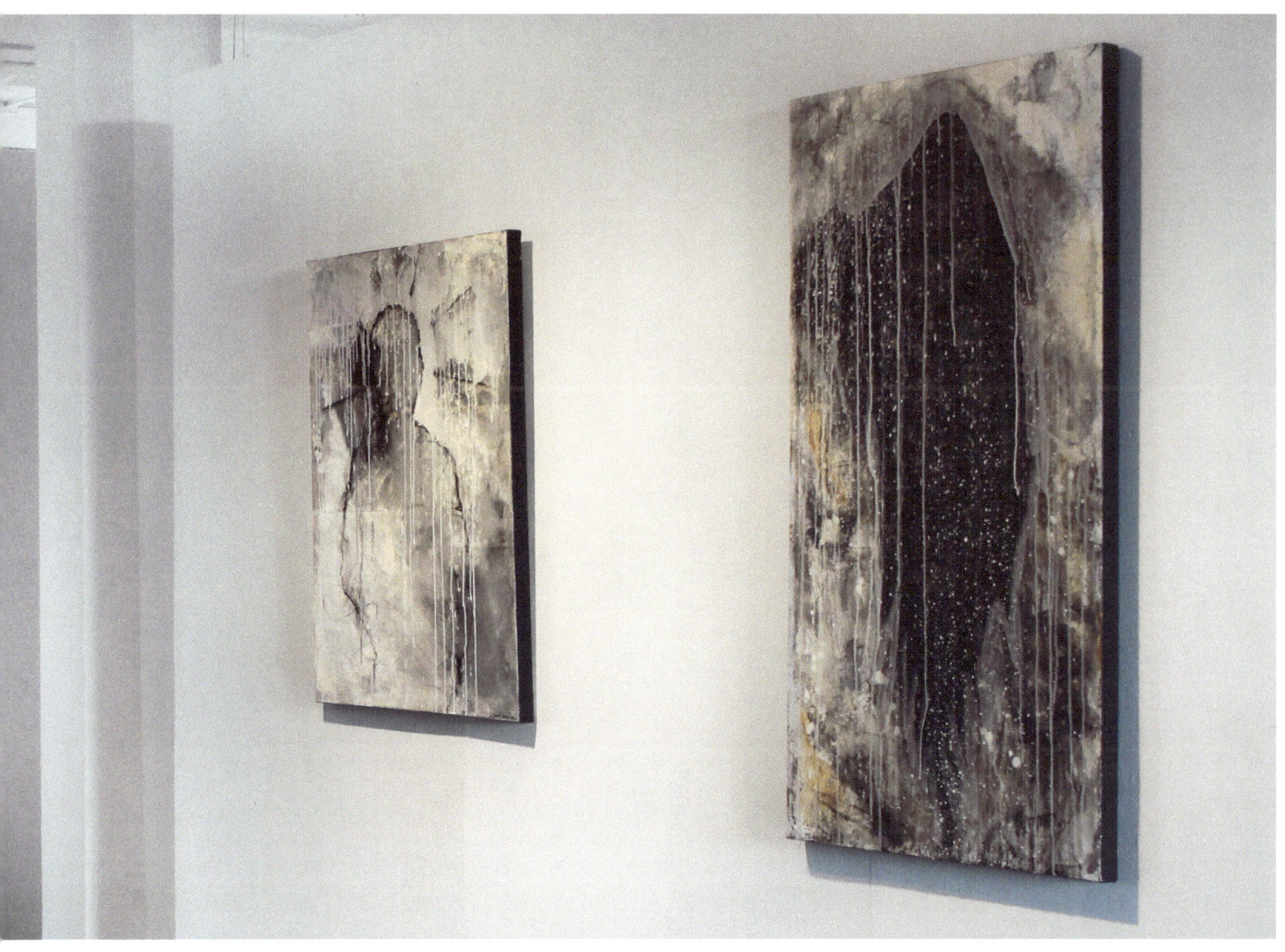

his art has our shared plight of suffering, of searching, and of triumph at its center. Far from a dualism that posits a separation between body and transcendence, Gomez's artful technique underscores how art points to the indissoluble unity of what is matter and what is spirit. In Gomez's work the use of multiple textures, visible seams, dripping paint, vibrant colors and brushstrokes honors corporality, as his evocative figures celebrate personhood and the world in which we dwell. Yet Gomez's works also act like modern icons opening windows and doors into the depths of Spirit, where death never has the last word and the sacred beckons."

"In his passionate and passion-making art Sergio Gomez tells a community's story, raises a cry of pain, mediates a vision of hope, and points with care and reverence toward that eternal Other whose love the very beauty of these works brings into relationship with a thankful world."

Cecilia González-Andrieu Ph.D.
Art/Religion/Theology/Spirituality
Loyola Marymount University | Los Angeles, CA
Bridge to Wonder: Art as a Gospel of Beauty
Waco: Baylor University Press, 2012, pages 157, 162

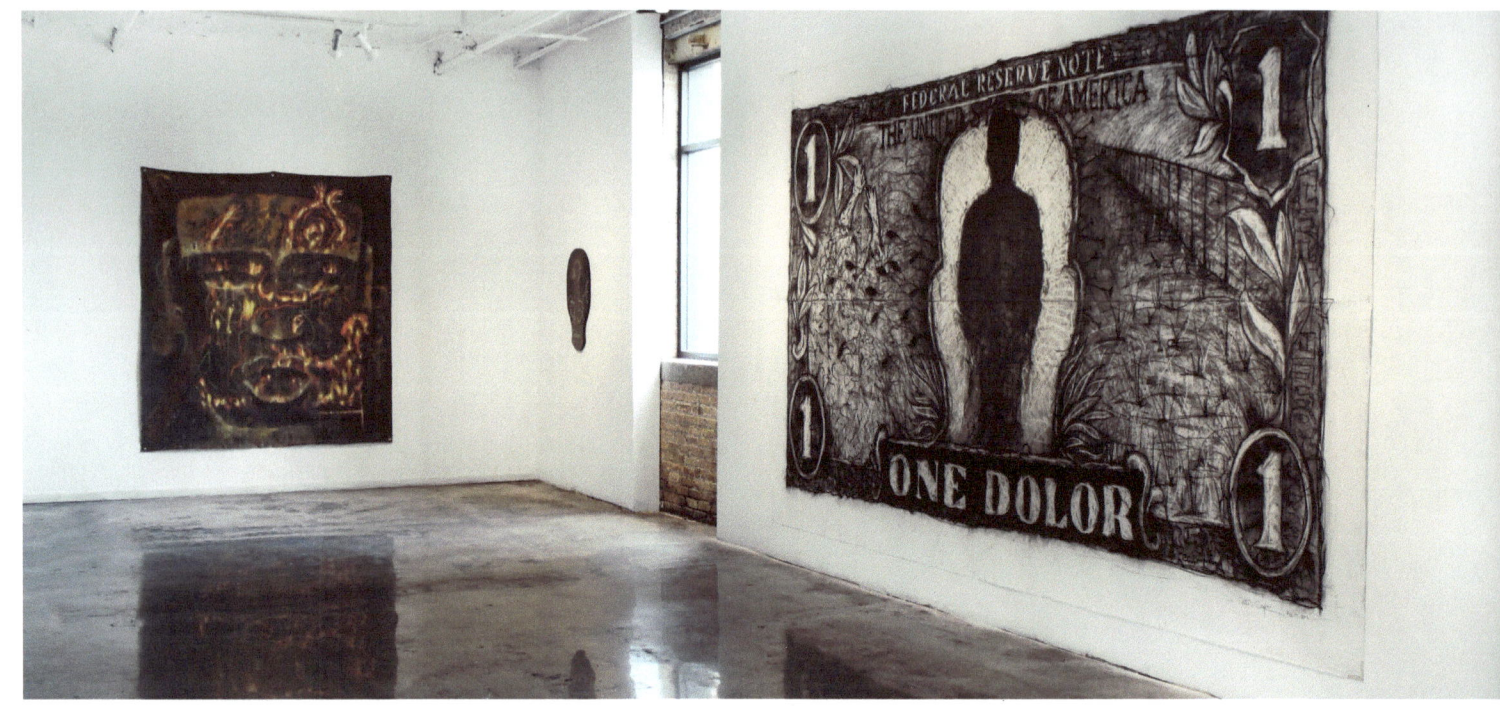

It Feels Like I Was Already Here
Sergio Gomez Solo Exhibition

Exhibitions Dates: August 19 to September 10, 2016
Location: Zhou B Art Center 1029 W. 35th St, Chicago, IL 60609

In It Feels Like I Was Already Here, Gomez presents his largest solo exhibition to date featuring painting and drawing works at the Zhou B Art Center where Sergio first established his studio and currently is curator and Director of Exhibitions.

"When first entering an exhibit of Sergio's work, it is experienced that the temporal world is his mental metaphor. The embodied qualities of visual language are there for broader interpretation and encouragement for the viewer. There, the artist enlists participation with the mysterious transcendental journey" Laura Frazier.

It Feels Like I Was Already Here combines Gomez's figurative abstraction paintings often reflecting on the human condition along with large-scale char-coal drawings exploring social issues such as immigration, poverty and the environment. Gomez's richly worked surfaces tracing the essence or impression of personhood provide a visual reminder of our corporal presence while evoking a sense of spiritual transcendence.

This exhibition presents Gomez as both an artist and curator simultaneously. His career for the last 11 years has been closely associated with the rise of the art community in Chicago's south side. Starting with Bridgeport Third Fridays, which Sergio established for the first time in November of 2004, to his many curatorial exhibitions that bring hundreds of visitors to the Zhou B Art Center each month, Gomez continues to push art forward in Chicago and abroad. He is also known for his entrepreneurial spirit and his continued efforts to build a sense of community wherever he goes.

"Sergio Gomez has played an important role in the development of the Zhou B Art Center. The Center started from nothing, bare bones to one of the most important art institutions and Sergio was instrumental in this development. He came in with a belief and the vision of what the Zhou B Art Center could and would be. He is the Director of exhibitions at the Zhou B Art Center and has curated hundreds of important shows, among them is the National Wet Paint MFA show and the Self Portrait show. He is a dedicated artist and sets an inspirational example for many young, aspiring and established artists through cultivation of his dedication, passion and love for art." Zhou Brothers.

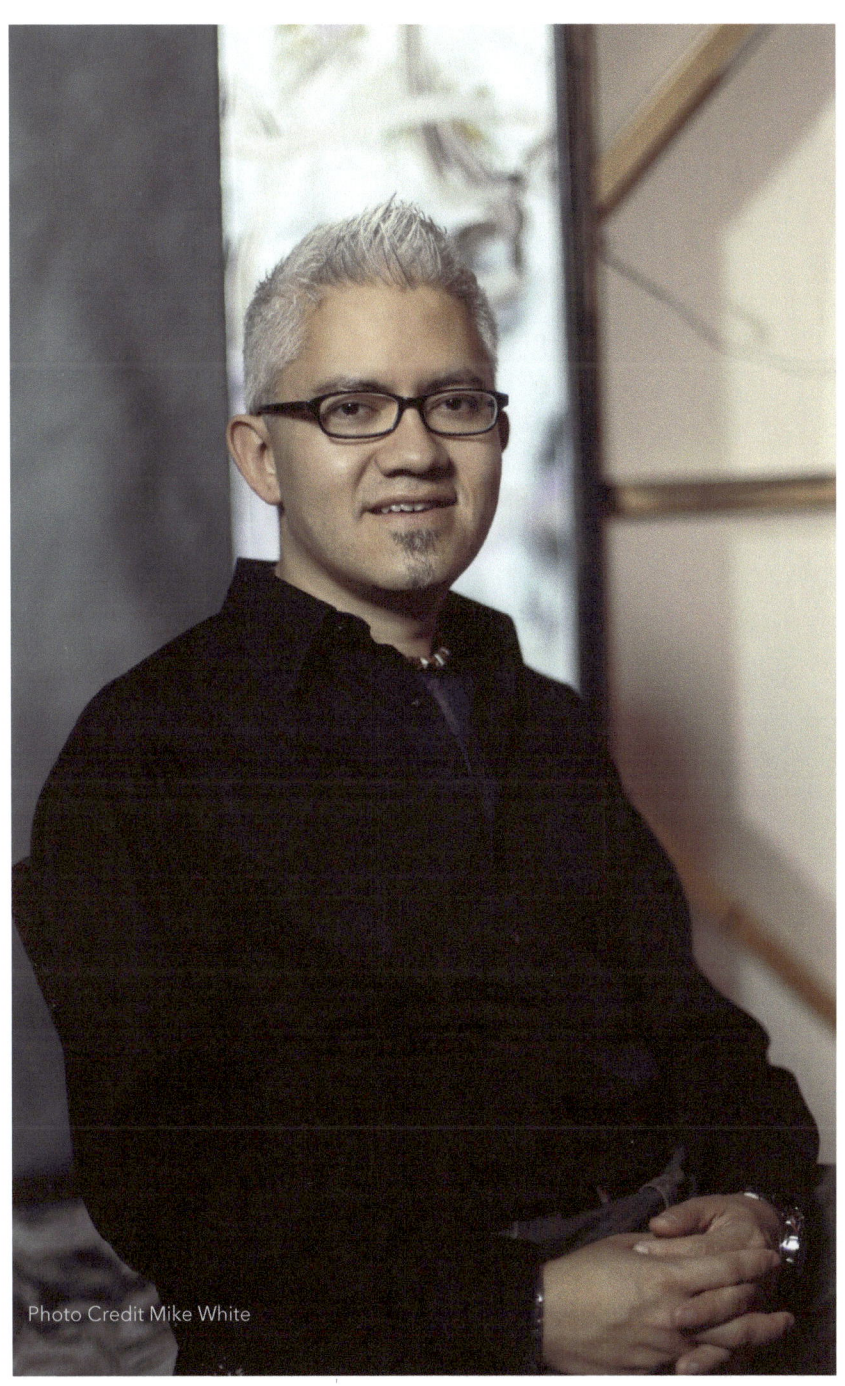
Photo Credit Mike White

About Sergio Gomez

Sergio Gomez is a Chicago based visual artist and creative entrepreneur. He received a Master of Fine Arts degree from Northern Illinois University. Sergio's work has been subject of solo exhibitions in the United States, Italy, Mexico and Vienna. He has participated in numerous group exhibitions in Spain, Sweden, Cairo, London, Korea, Mexico and the US. His work can be found in private and public collections of the National Museum of Mexican Art, Brauer Art Museum, and the MIIT Museo Internazionale Italia Arte among other public and private collections.

Currently, Sergio Gomez is the owner and director of 33 Contemporary Gallery, Curator/Director of Exhibitions at the Zhou B. Art Center, contributor for Italia Arte Magazine, Art/Design faculty at South Suburban College, Creative Consultant for Idea Seat Marketing and Advertising, co-founder of the Art NXT Level Strategic Community and founder of Amplified Art Network. His weekly Artist Next Level podcast inspires and educates contemporary artists. Sergio has curated special projects for the Chicago Park District, ArtSpot Miami International Art Fair during Art Basel Miami (2013, 2014), National Museum of Mexican Art, and ExpoChicago (2014) among others. web: sergiogomezonline.com

About the Zhou B Art Center

The Zhou B Art Center was founded in 2004 by the internationally acclaimed Zhou Brothers. Located in Bridgeport, the Zhou B Art Center's mission is to promote and facilitate a cultural dialogue by organizing contemporary art exhibitions and programs of international scope. As a Center created by artists, for artists, the vision of the Center is to facilitate the exchange of contemporary art between Chicago and the international art community and promote the convergence of Eastern and Western art forms in the United States.

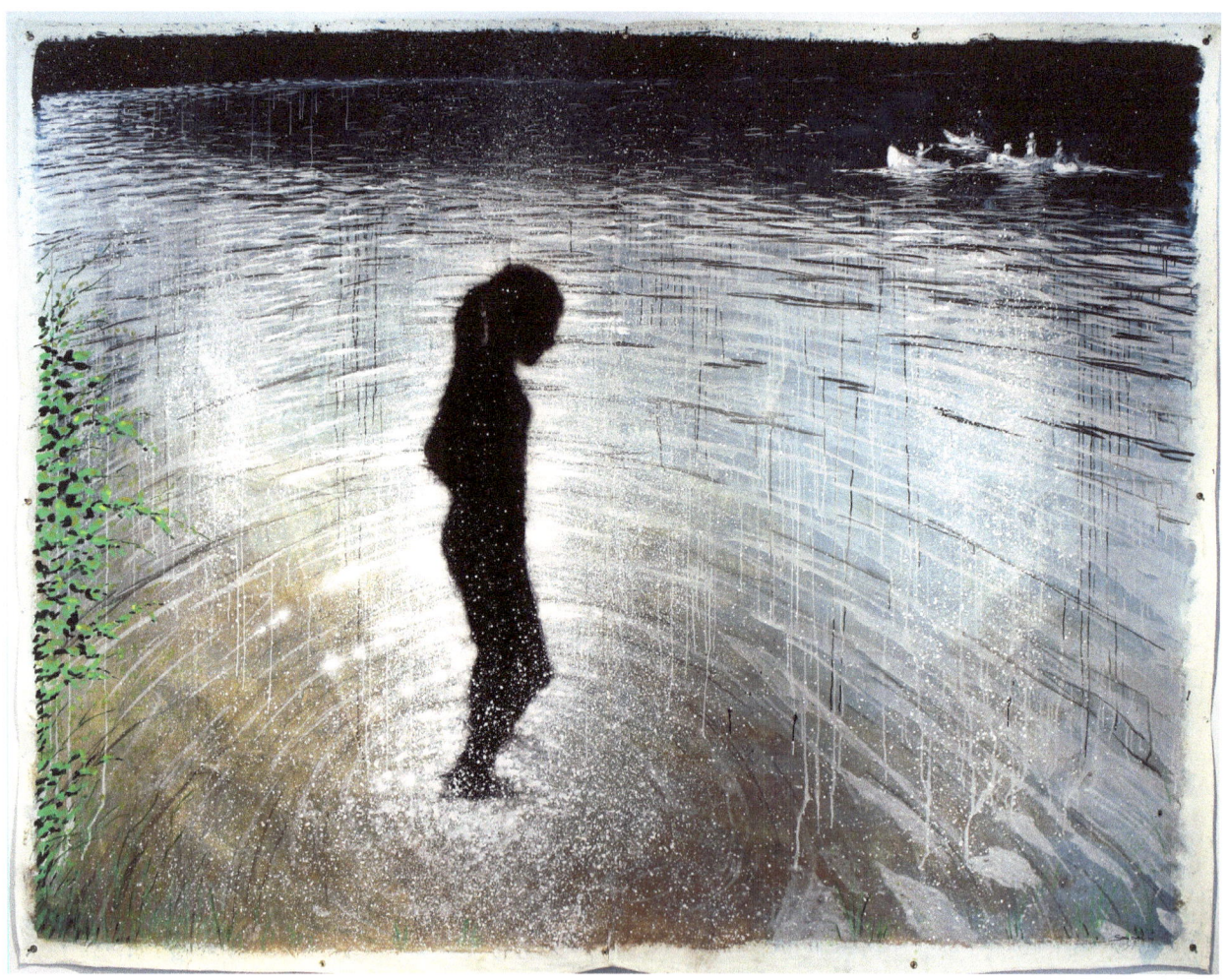

Walking on Water
Medium: Acrylic on Canvas
Size: 108 x 144 in

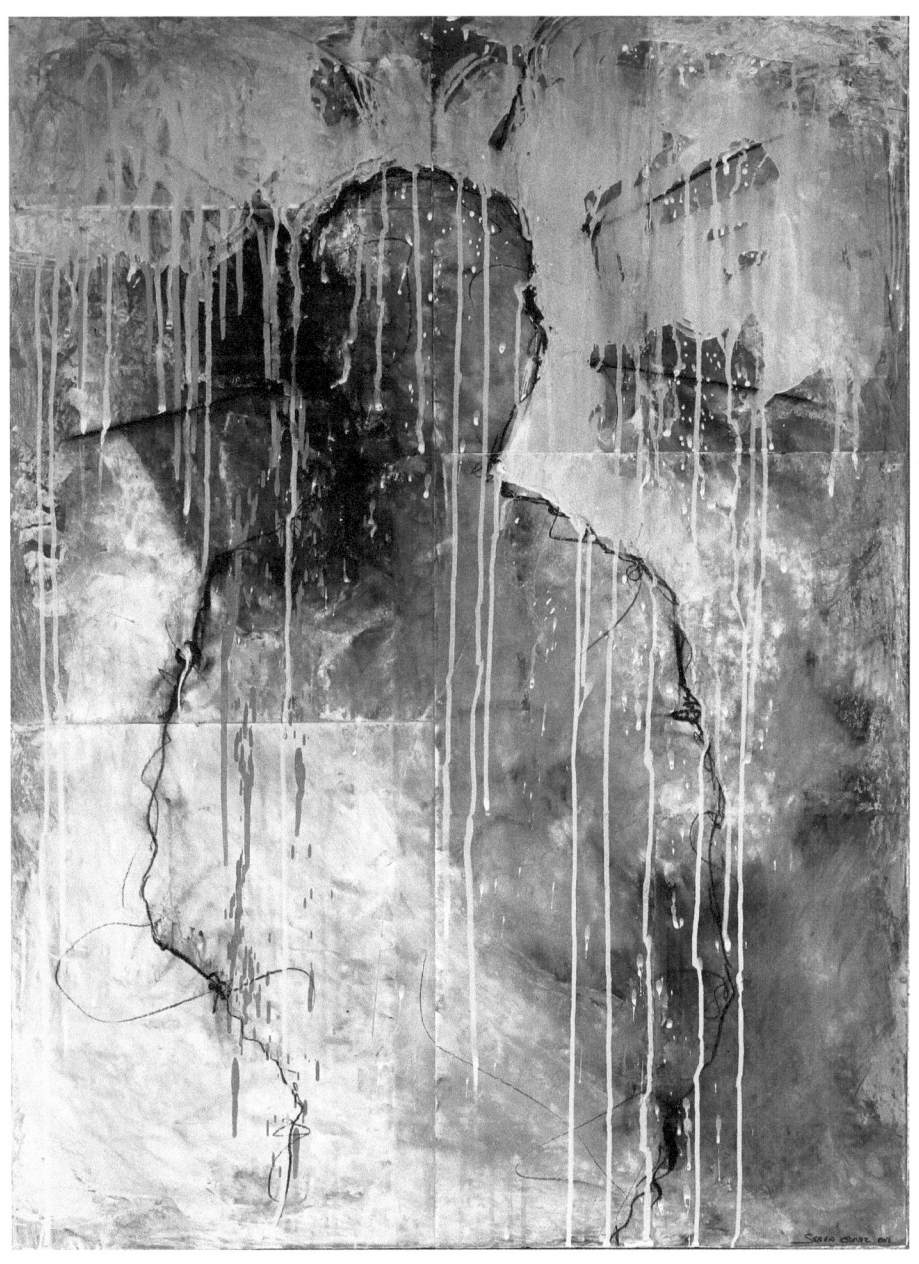

Reflection
Medium: Acrylic on Canvas
Size: 30 x 24 x 2 in

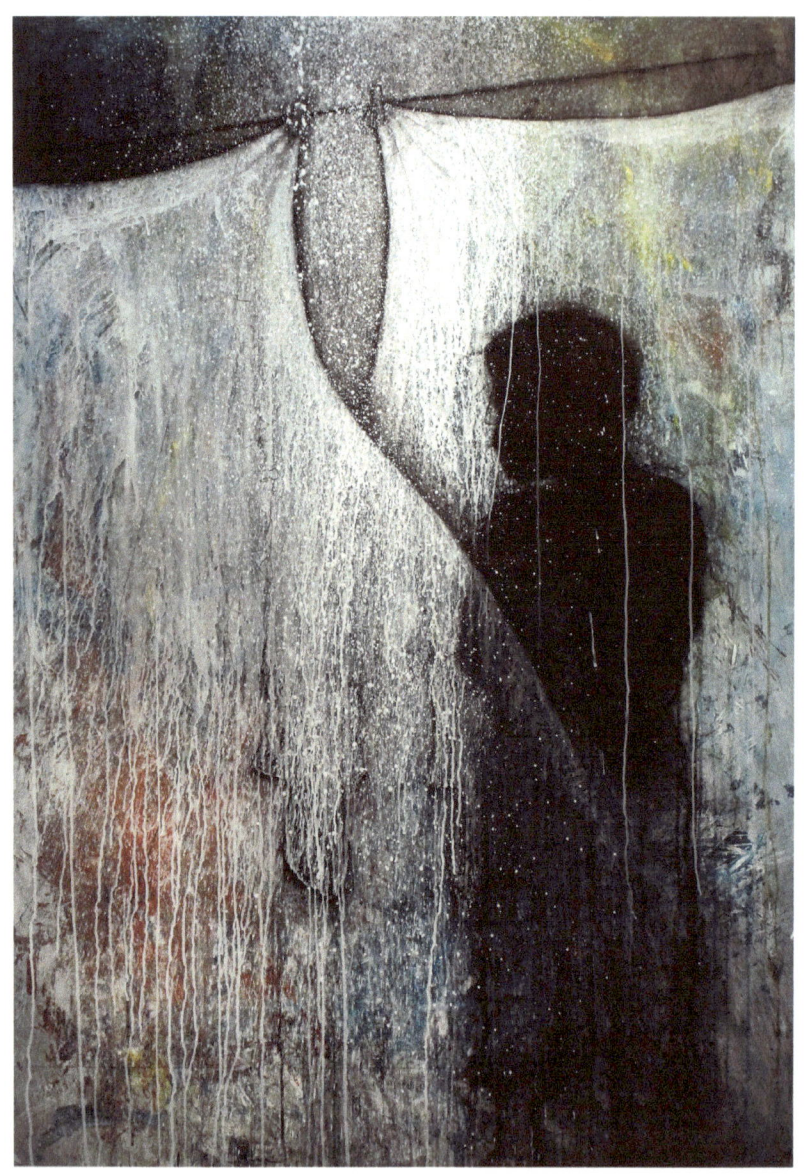

Consciousness
Medium: Acrylic on Canvas
Size: 71 x 51 x 0.5 in

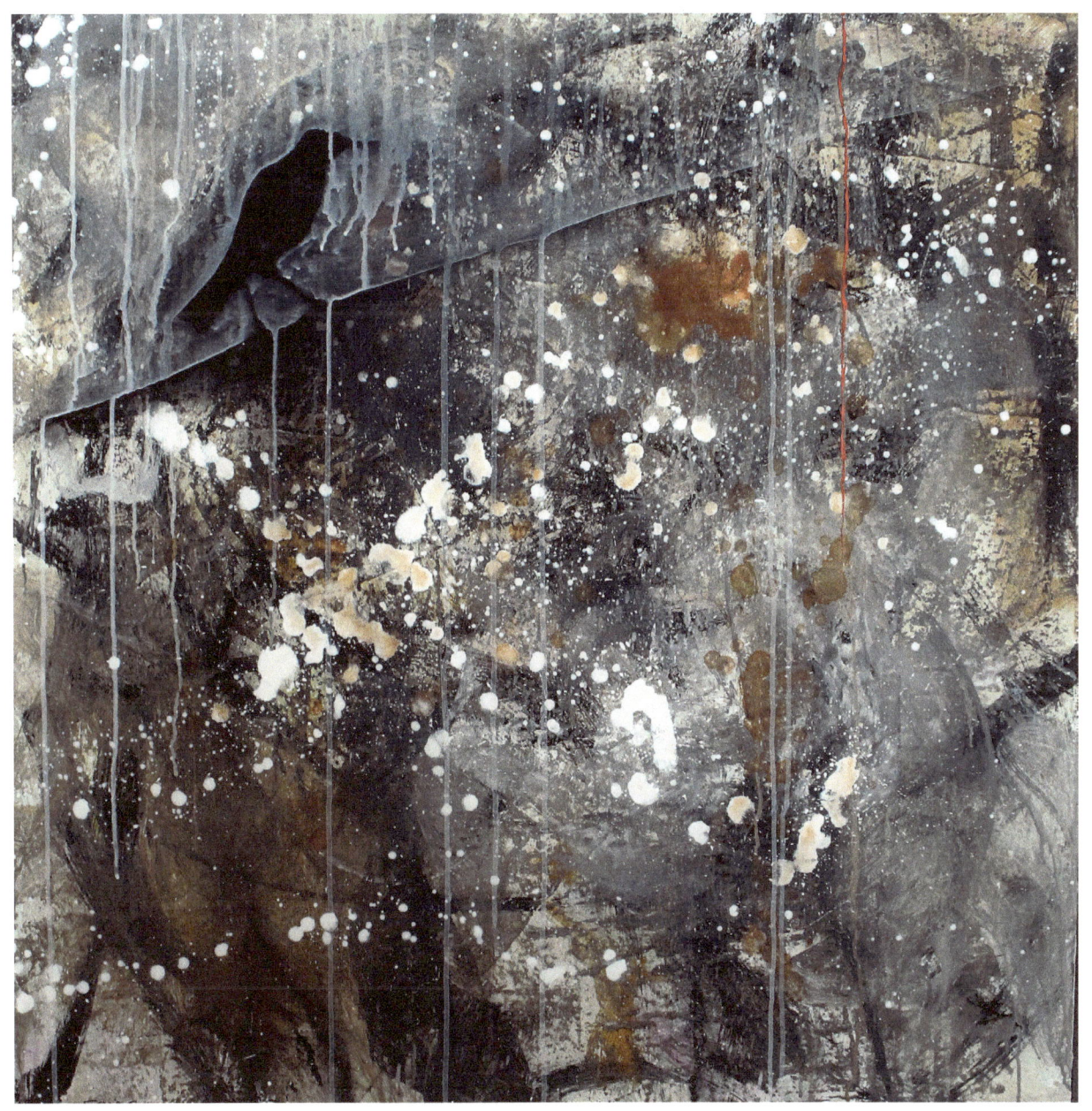

Declaration #1
Medium: Acrylic and charcoal on canvas
Size: 29.5 x 29.5 x 1 in

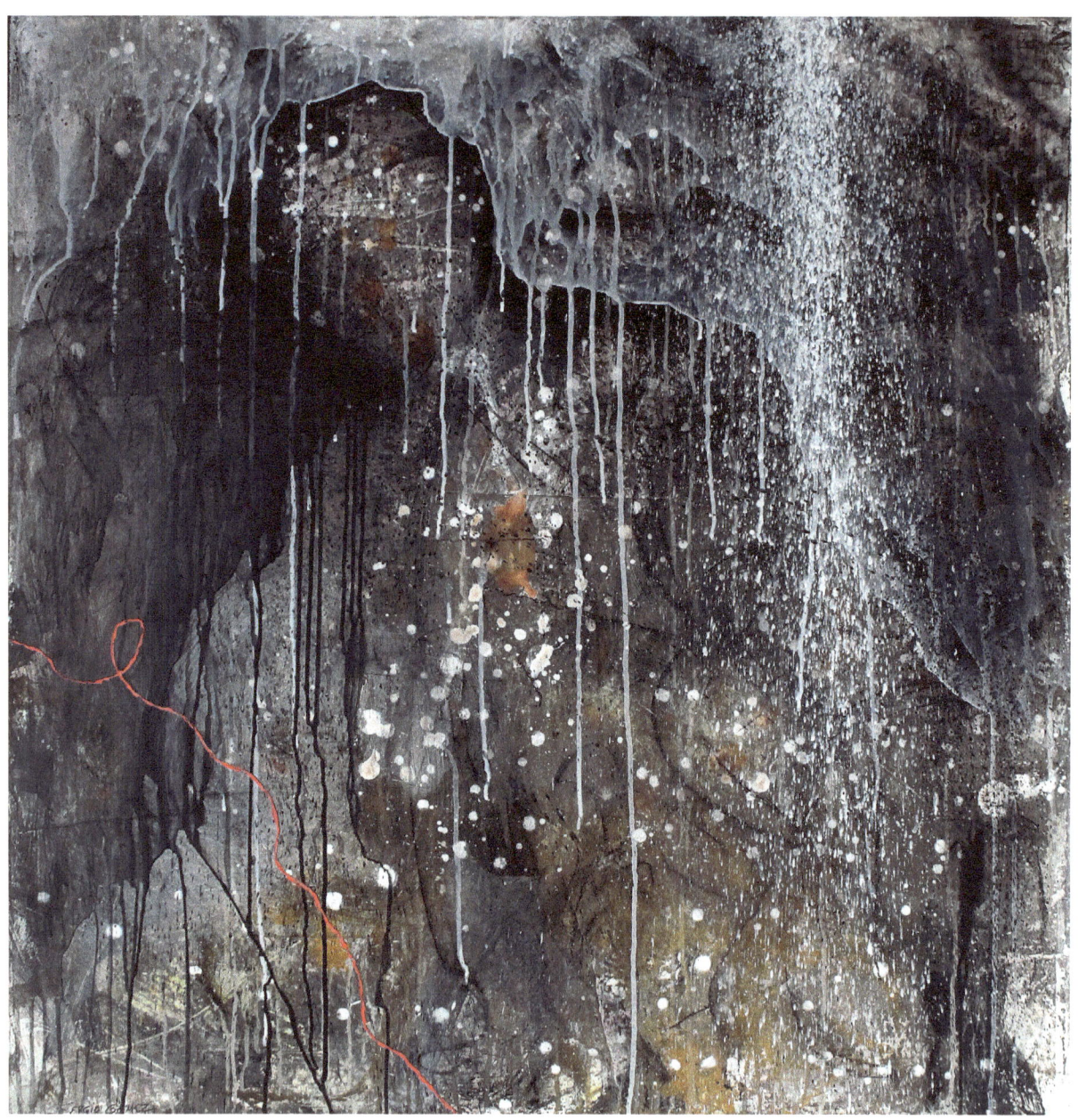

Declaration #2
Medium: Acrylic and charcoal on canvas
Size: 29.5 x 29.5 x 1 in

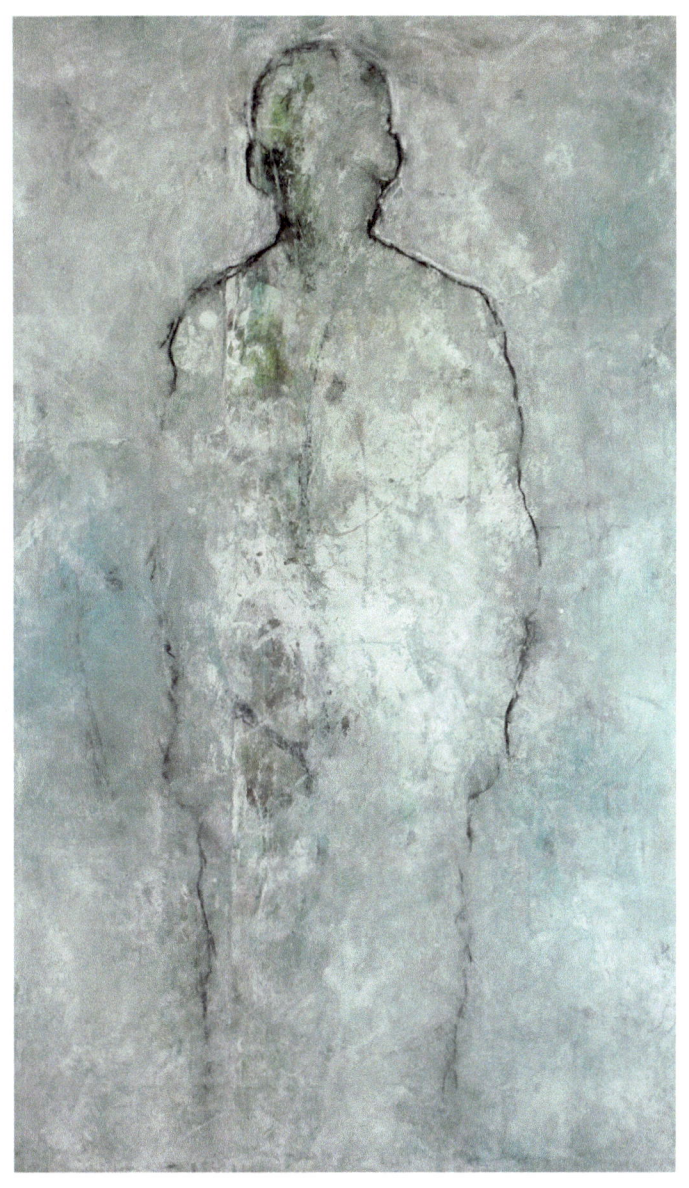

Healing #1
Medium: Acrylic and charcoal on paper / canvas
Size: 82 x 42 in

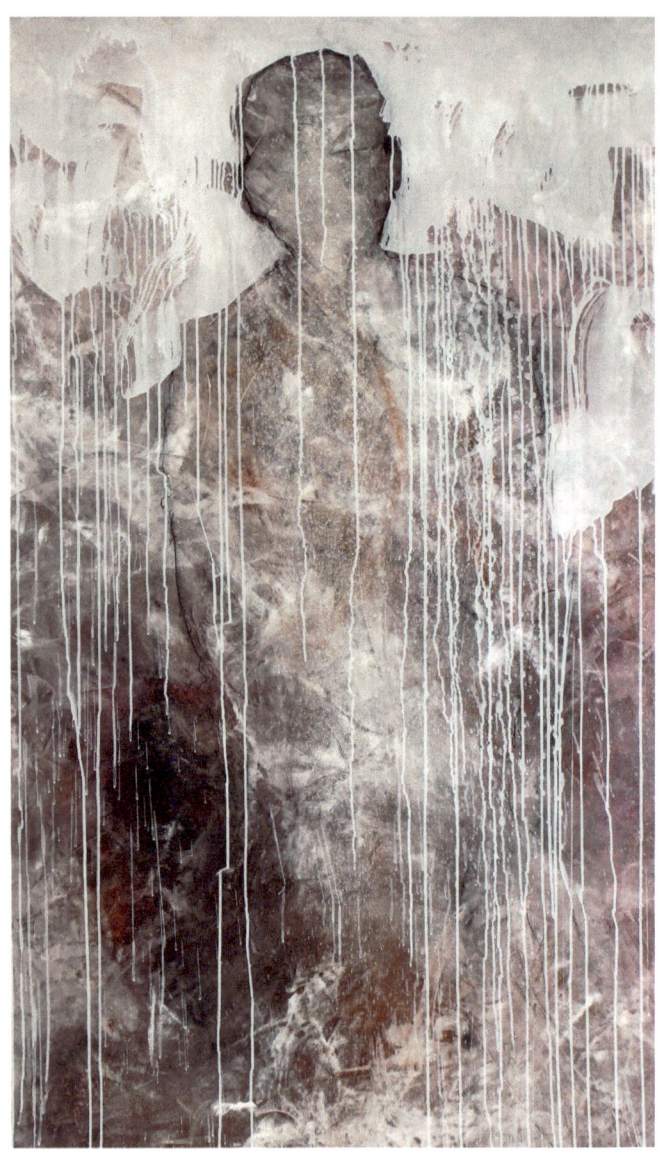

Healing #2
Medium: Acrylic and charcoal on paper / canvas
Size: 82 x 42 in

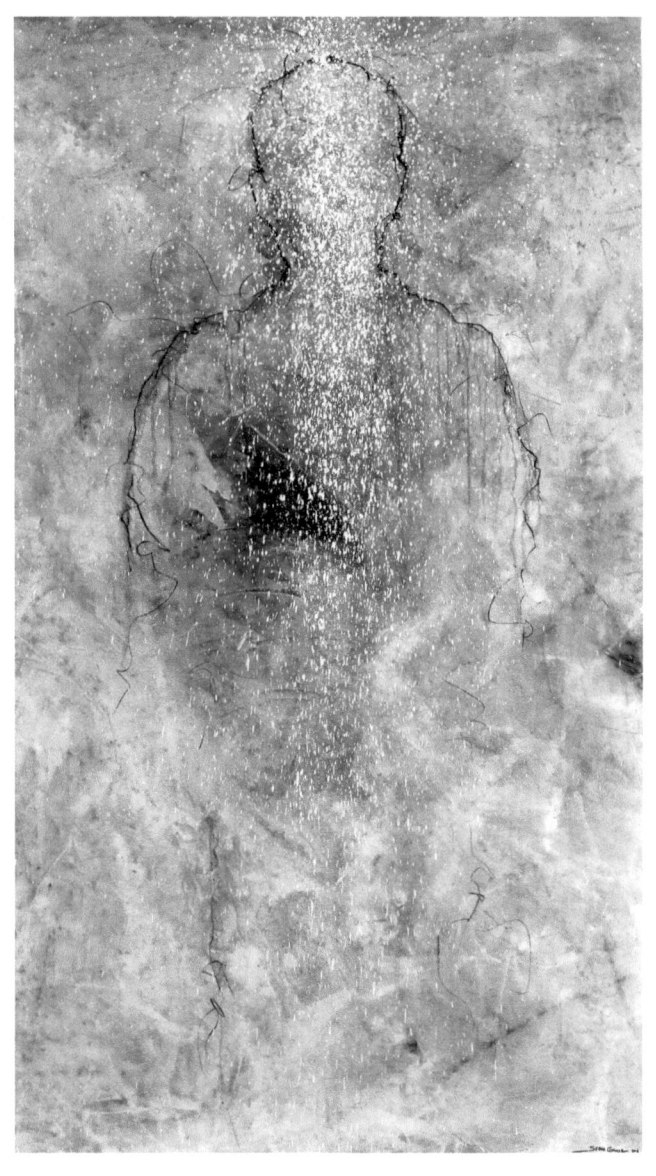

Healing #3
Medium: Acrylic and charcoal on paper / canvas
Size: 82 x 42 in

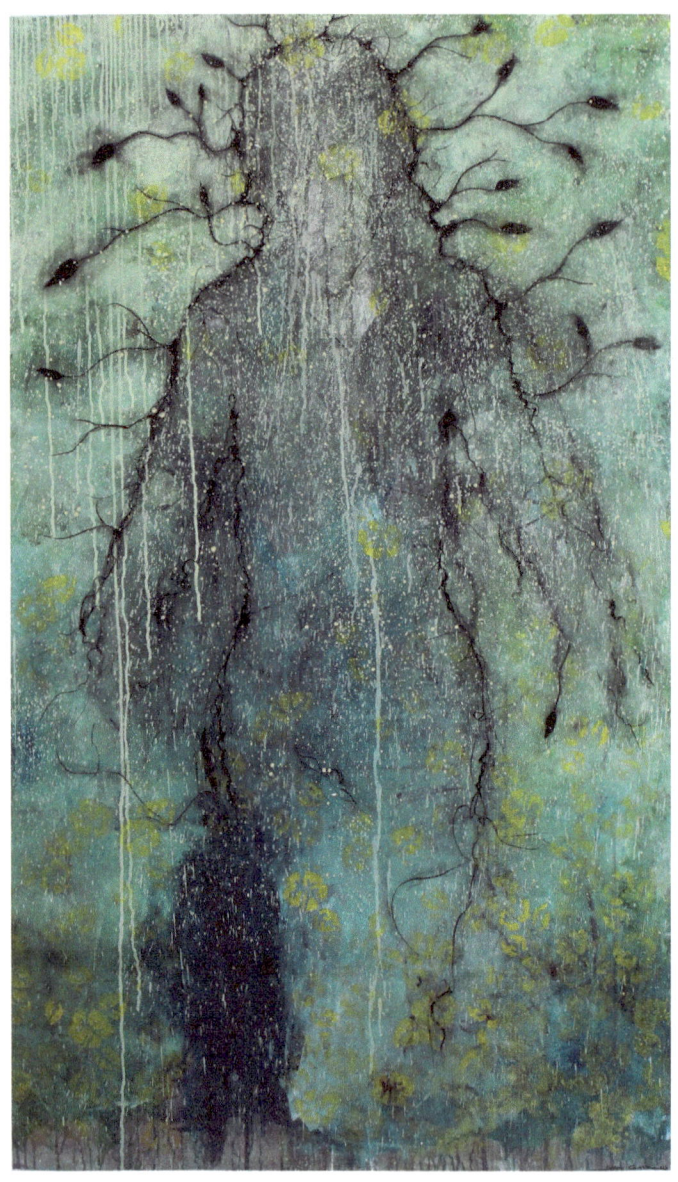

Healing #4
Medium: Acrylic and charcoal on paper /
canvas
Size: 82 x 42 in

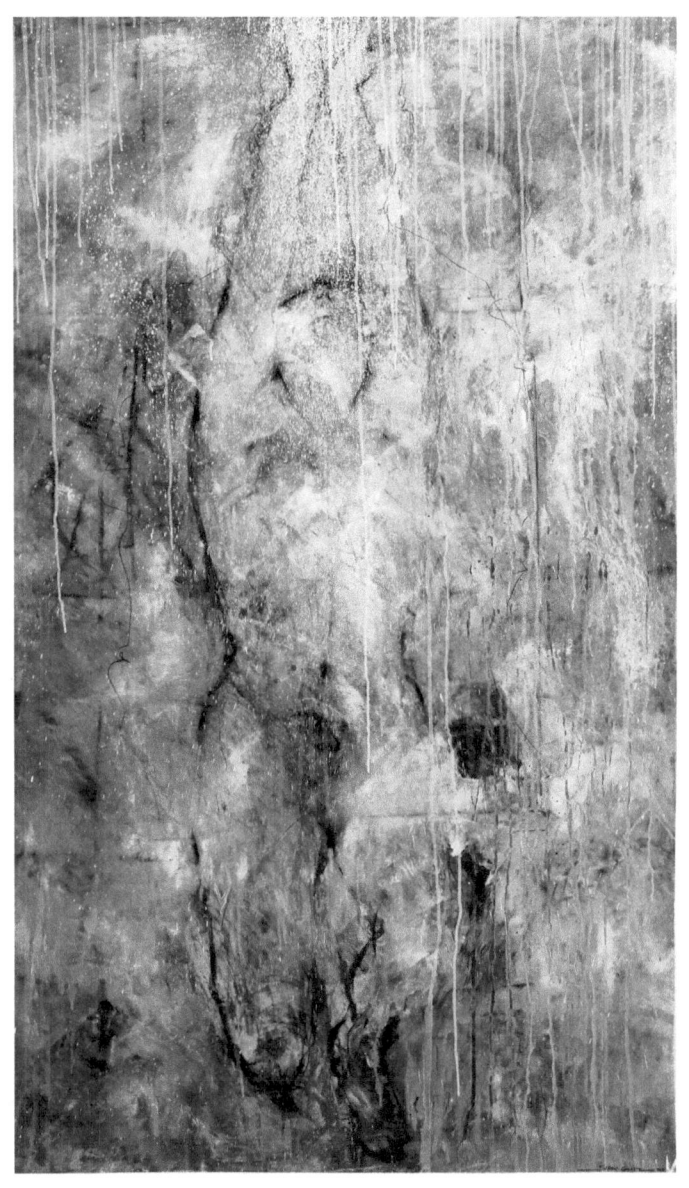

Healing #5
Medium: Acrylic and charcoal on paper / canvas
Size: 82 x 42 in

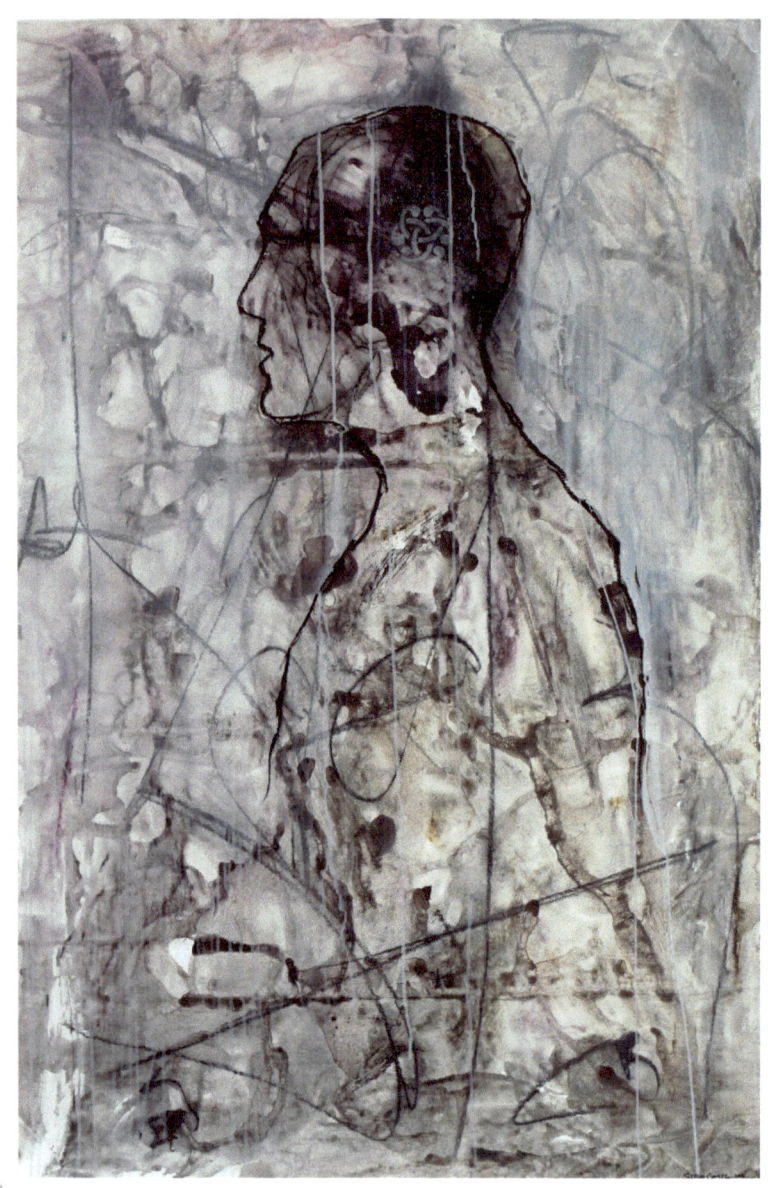

Healing #6
Medium: Acrylic on Paper/Canvas
Size: 82 x 42 in

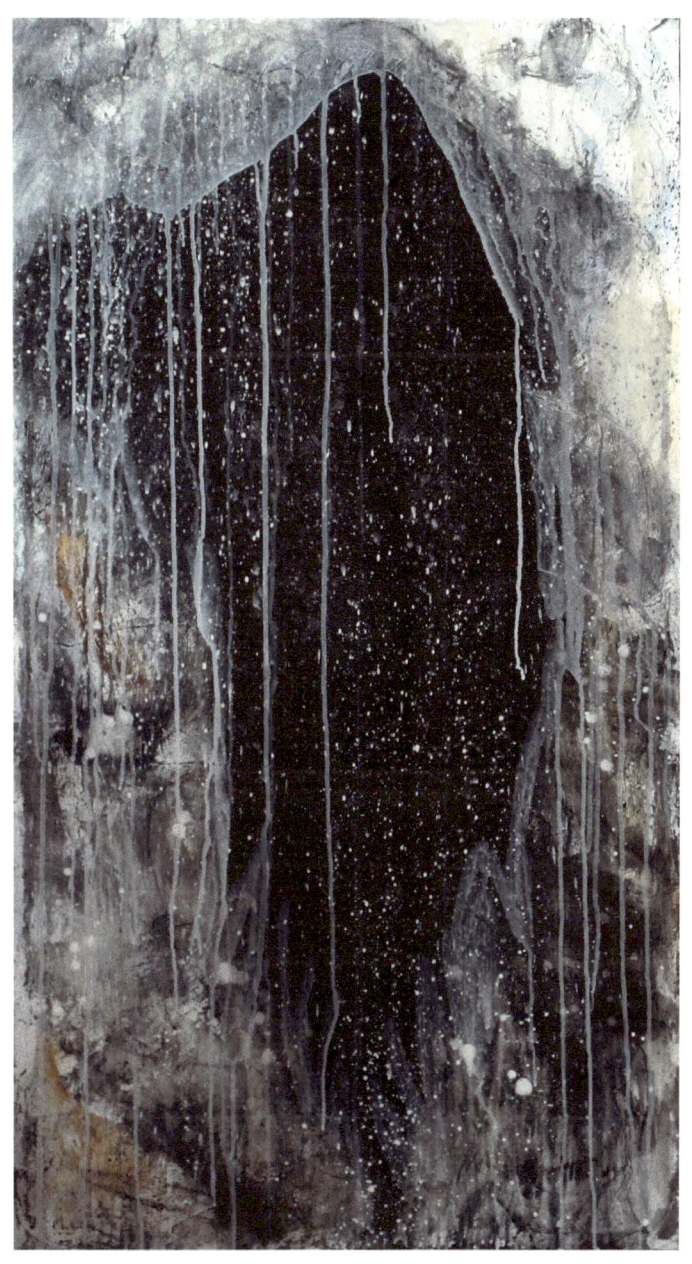

In the Shadow of Your Wing
Medium: Acrylic and charcoal on canvas
Size: 53 x 29 x 1 in

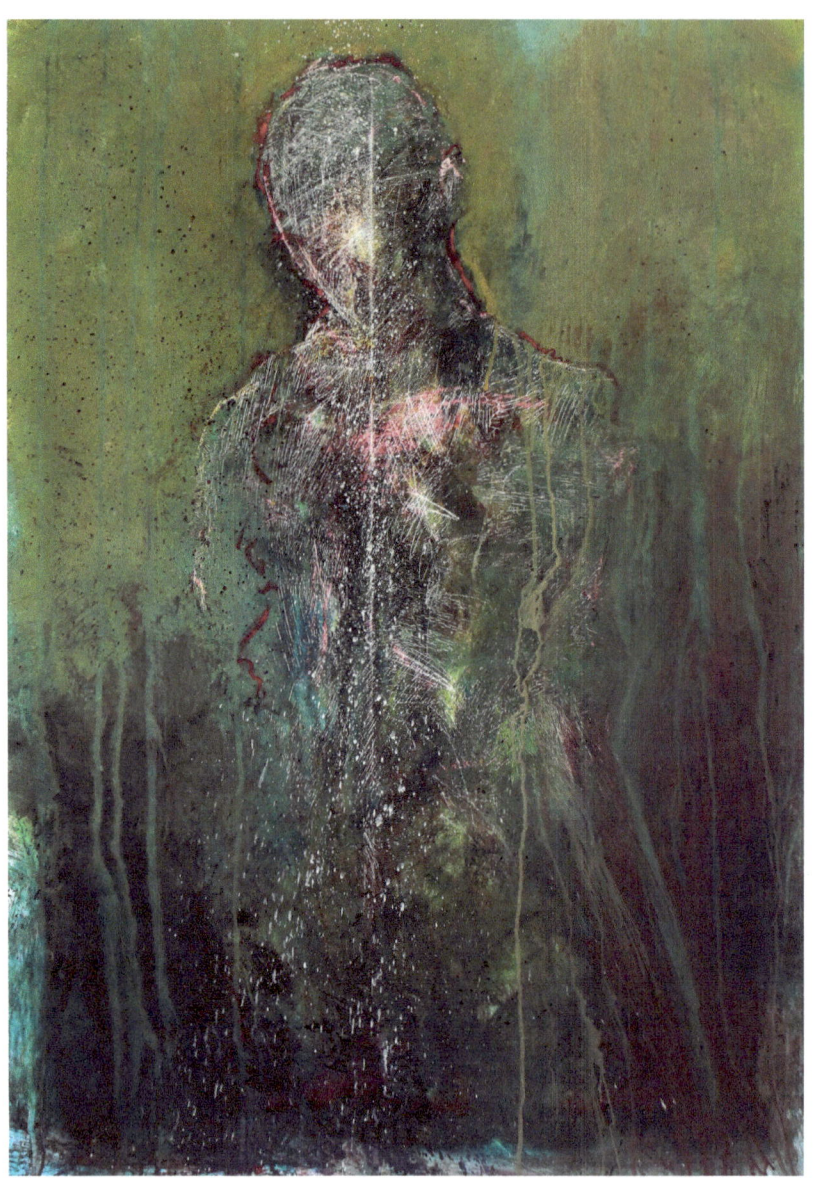

Searching in the Field of Light II
Medium: Acrylic on Canvas and Paper
Size: 50 x 36 in

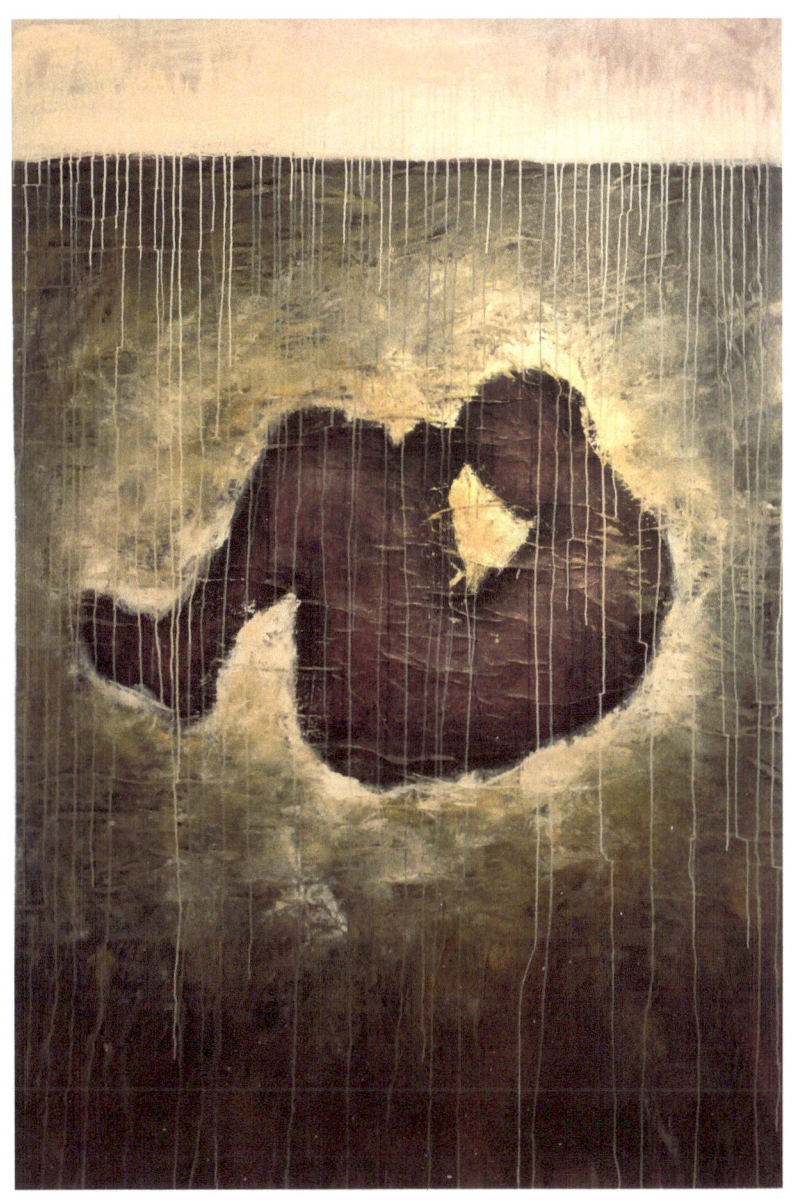

Tierra
Medium: Acrylic on Paper/Canvas
Size: 90 x 64 in

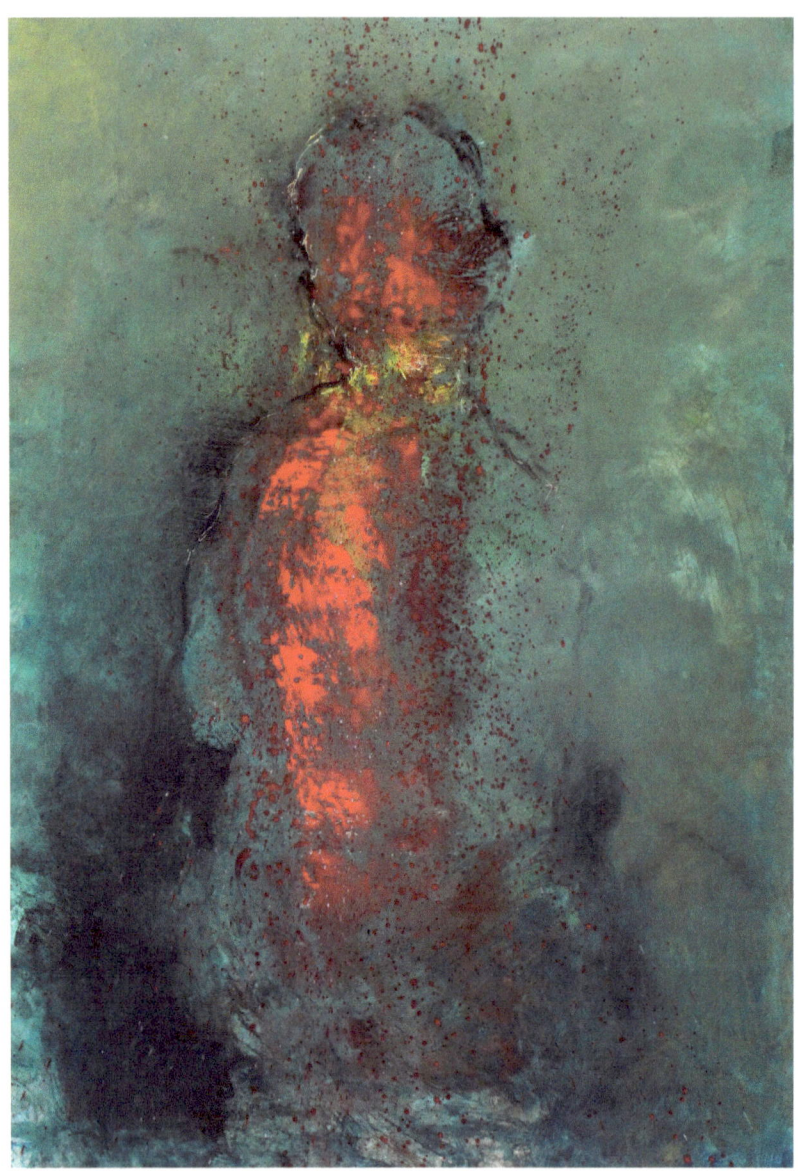

Searching in the Field of Light IV
Medium: Acrylic on Canvas and Paper
Size: 59 x 36 in

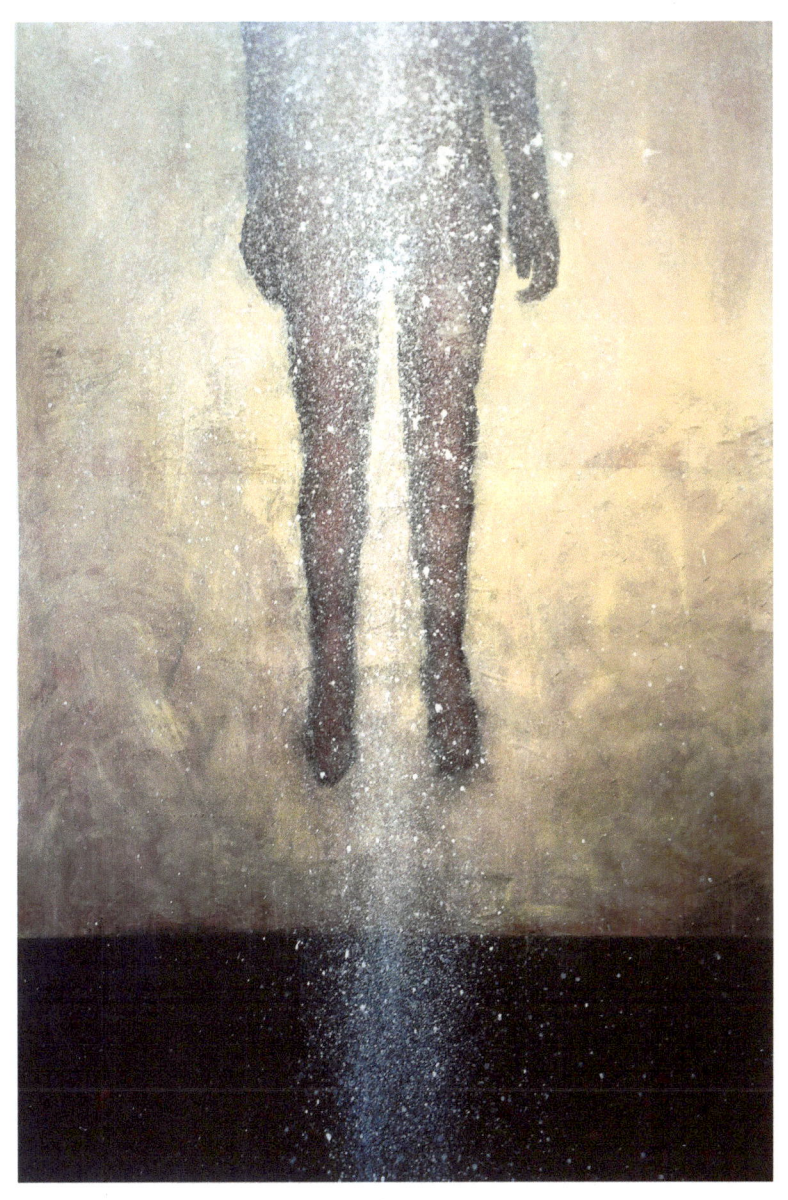

Aire
Medium: Acrylic on Paper/Canvas
Size: 90 x 64 in

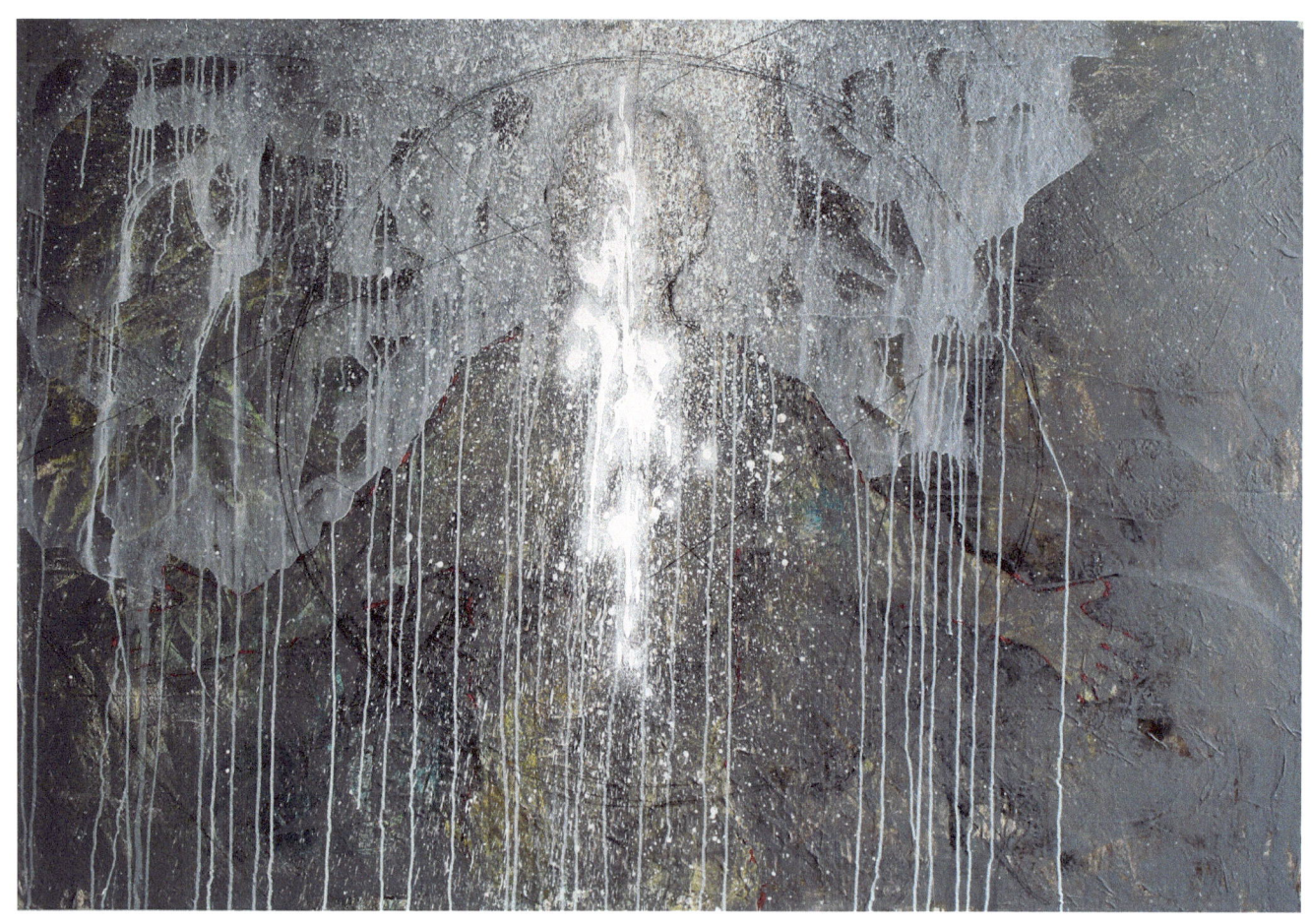

Balance
Medium: Acrylic on Canvas
Size: 48 x 72 x 2 in

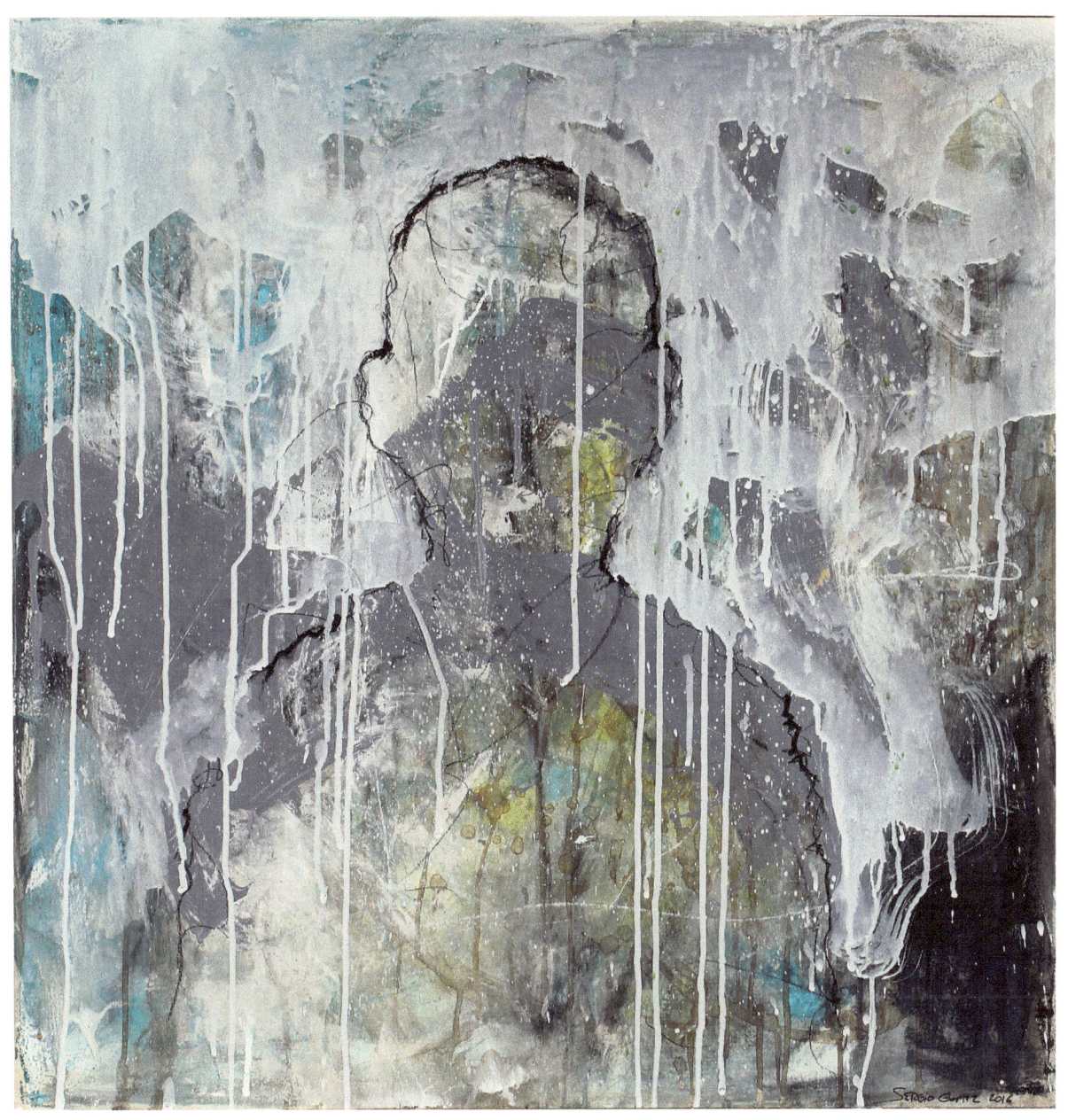

Serenity
Medium: Acrylic on Canvas
Size: 30 x 30 x 2 in

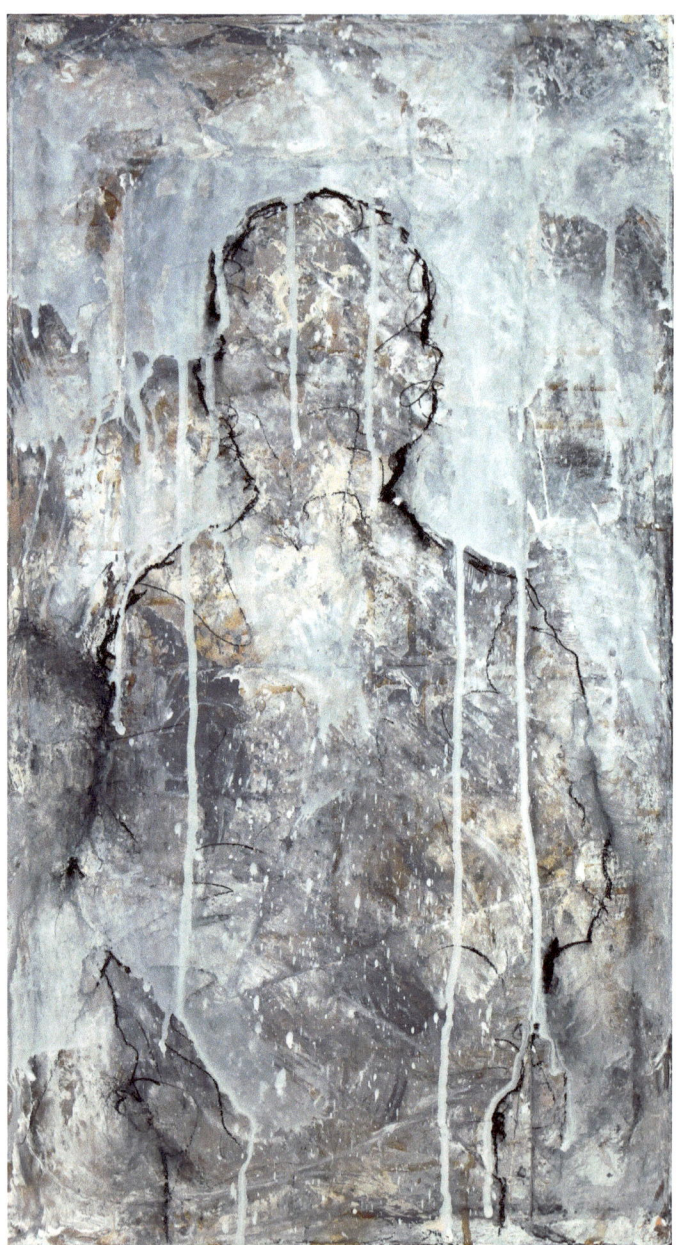

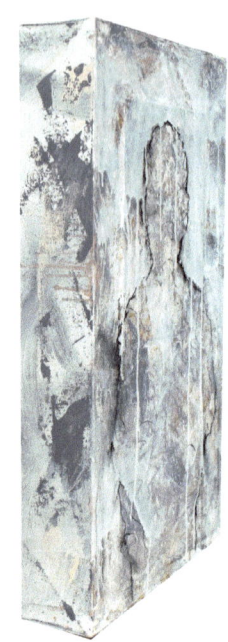

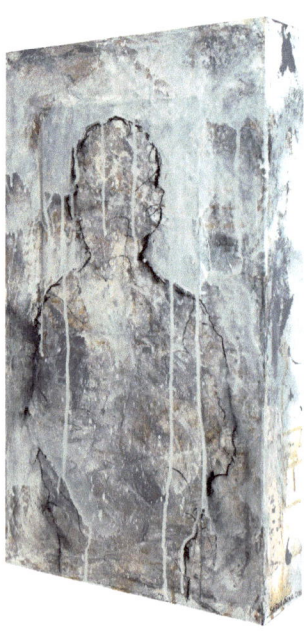

Fossil #2
Medium: Acrylic on Canvas
Size: 24 x 12 x 4 in

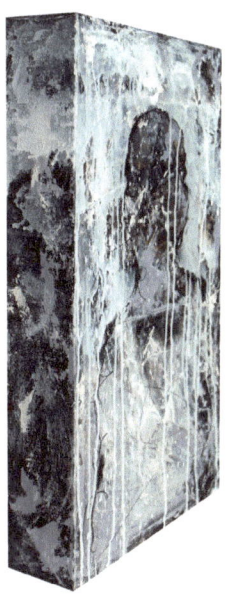

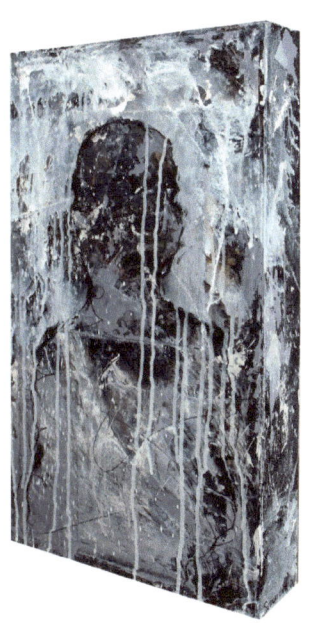

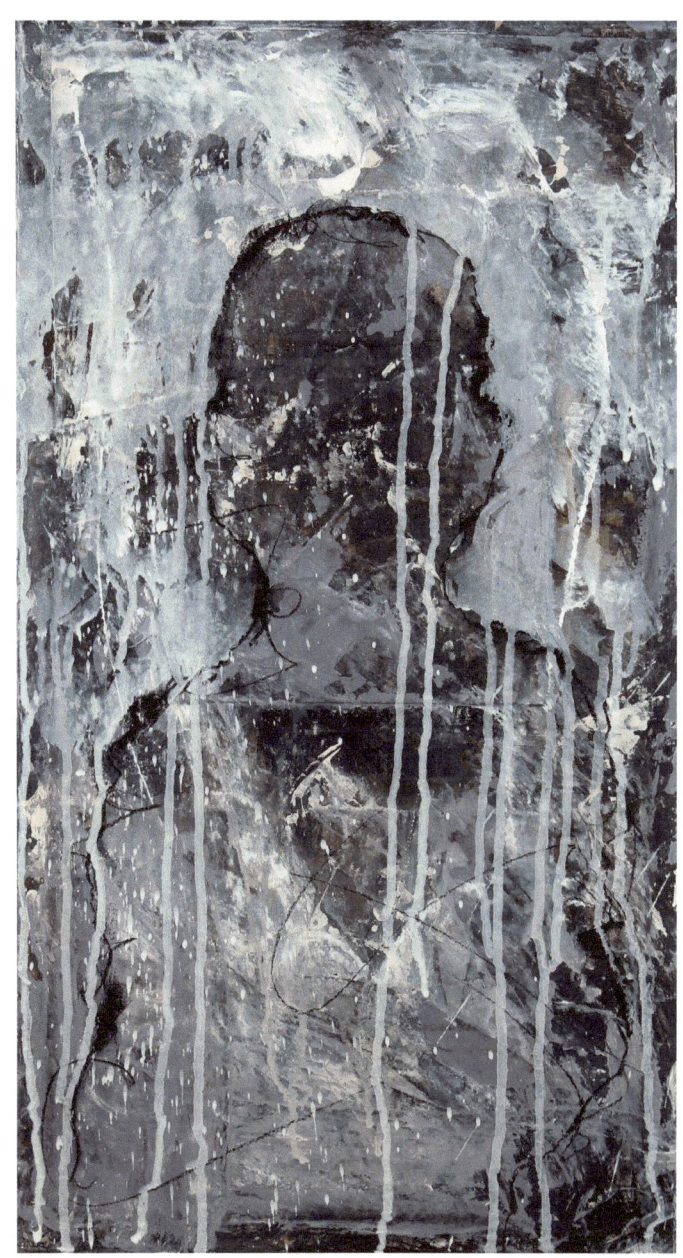

Fossil #1
Medium: Acrylic on Canvas
Size: 24 x 12 x 4 in

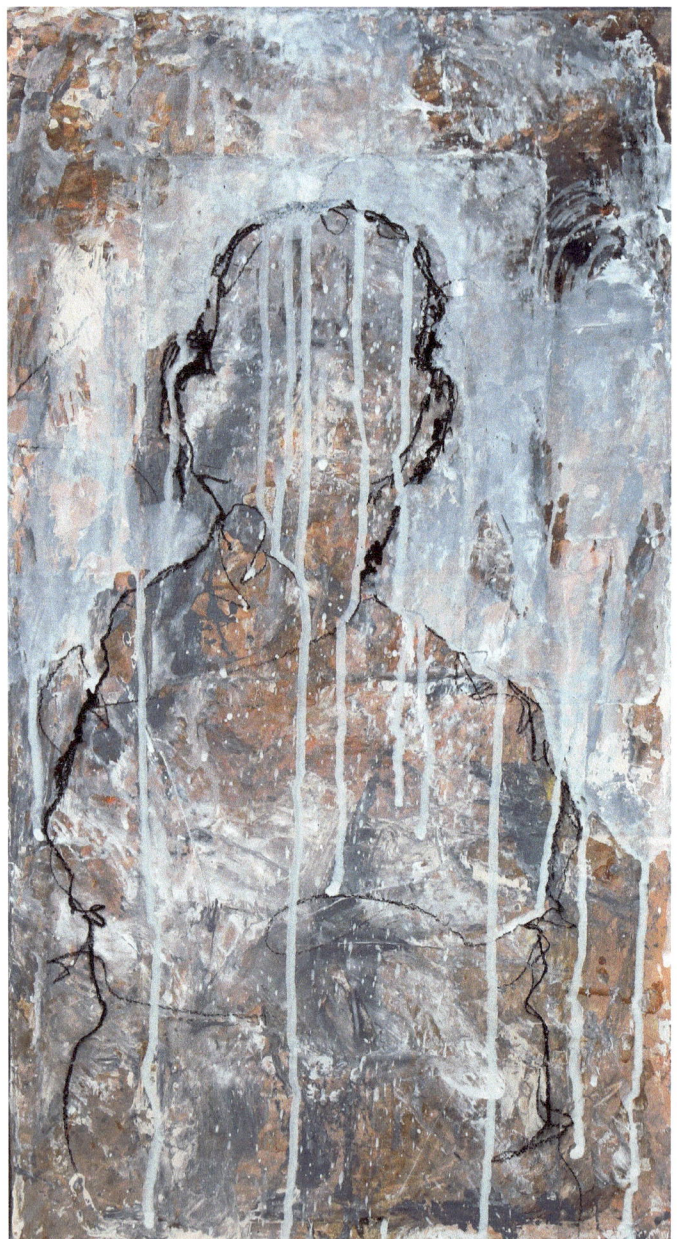

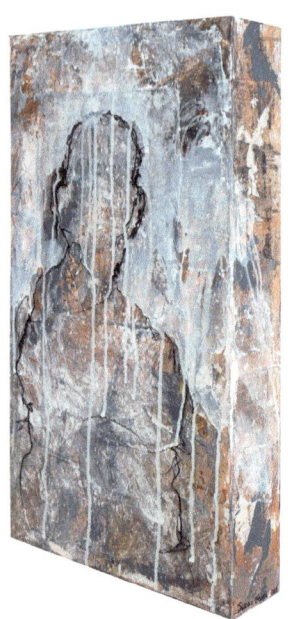

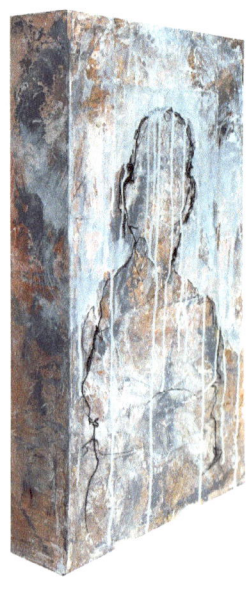

Fossil #3
Medium: Acrylic on Canvas
Size: 24 x 12 x 4 in

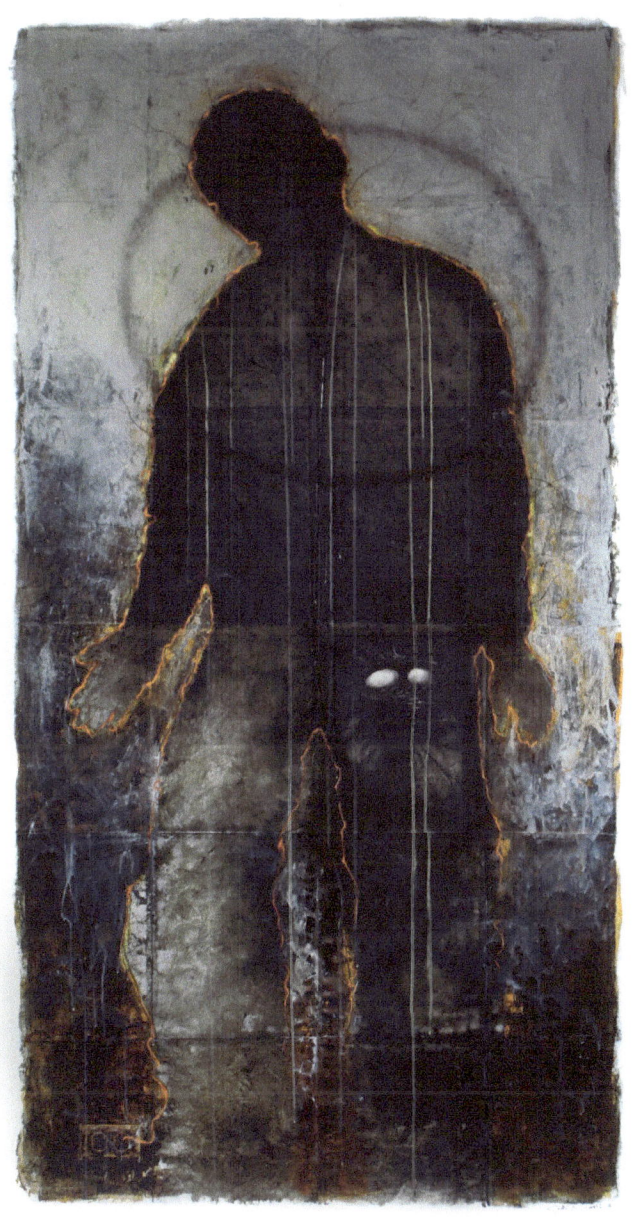

Vulnerable Man
Medium: Acrylic on paper/canvas
Size: 44 x 84 in

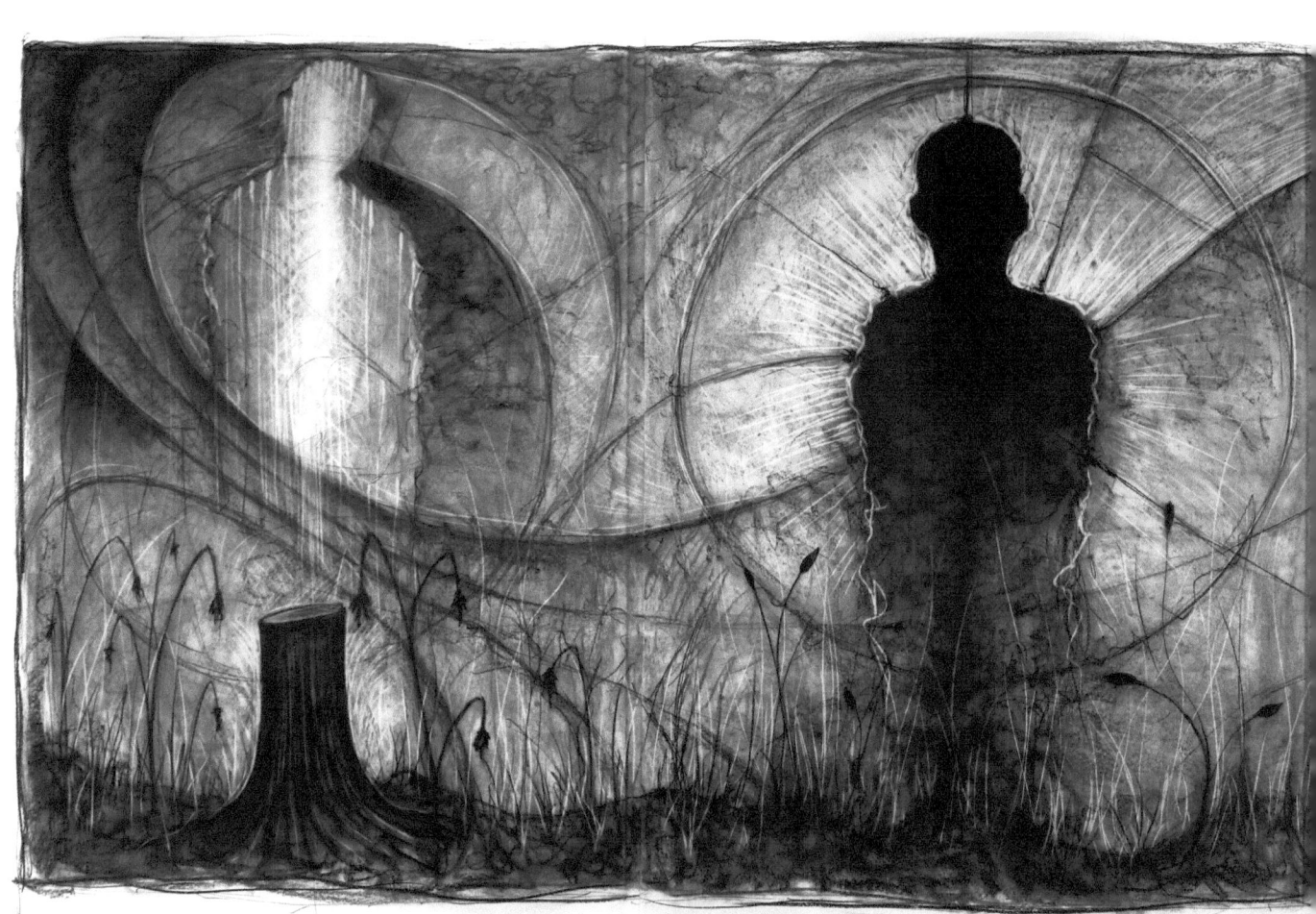

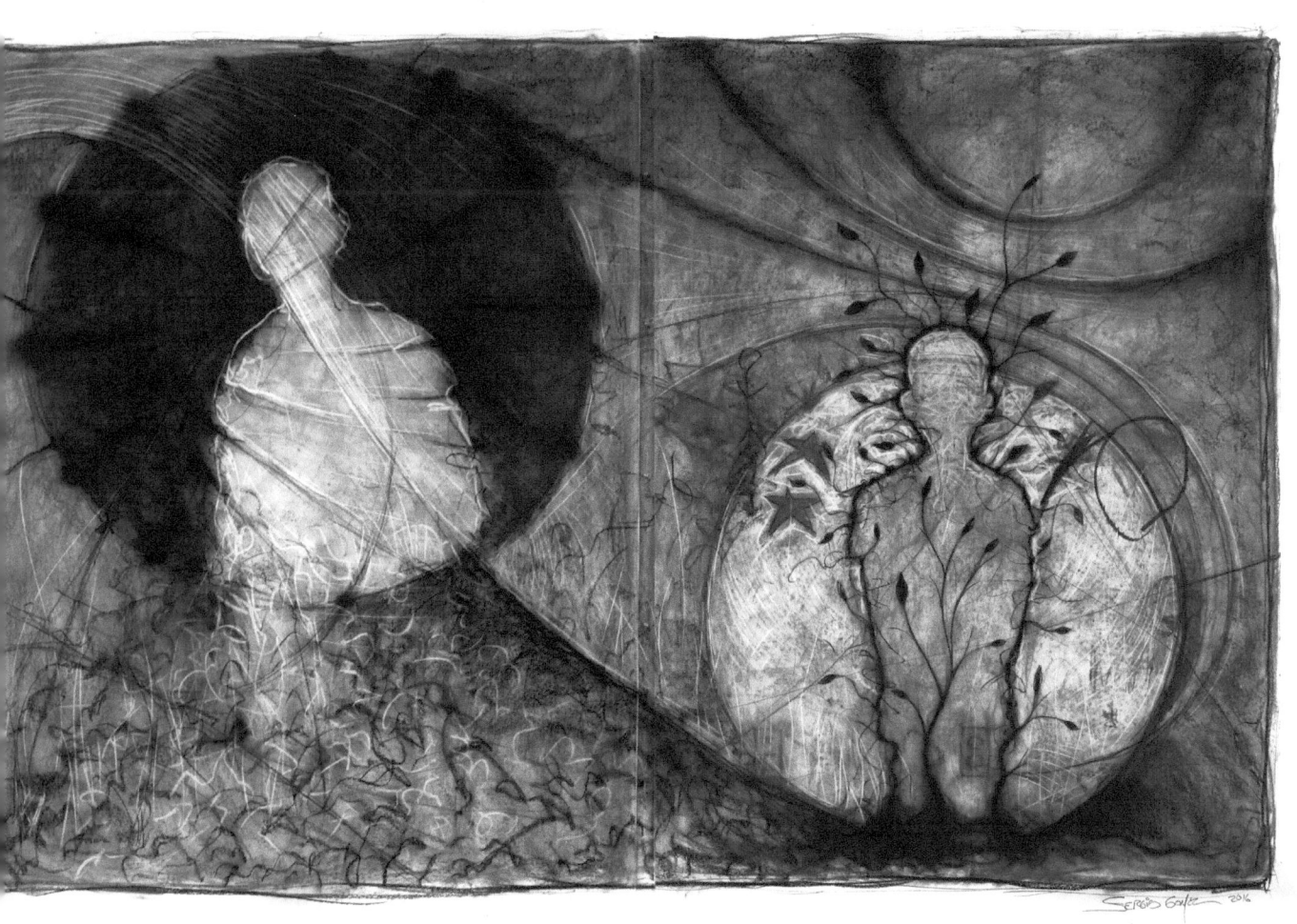

Life's Cycle
Medium: Charcoal on paper
Size: 96 x 237 in

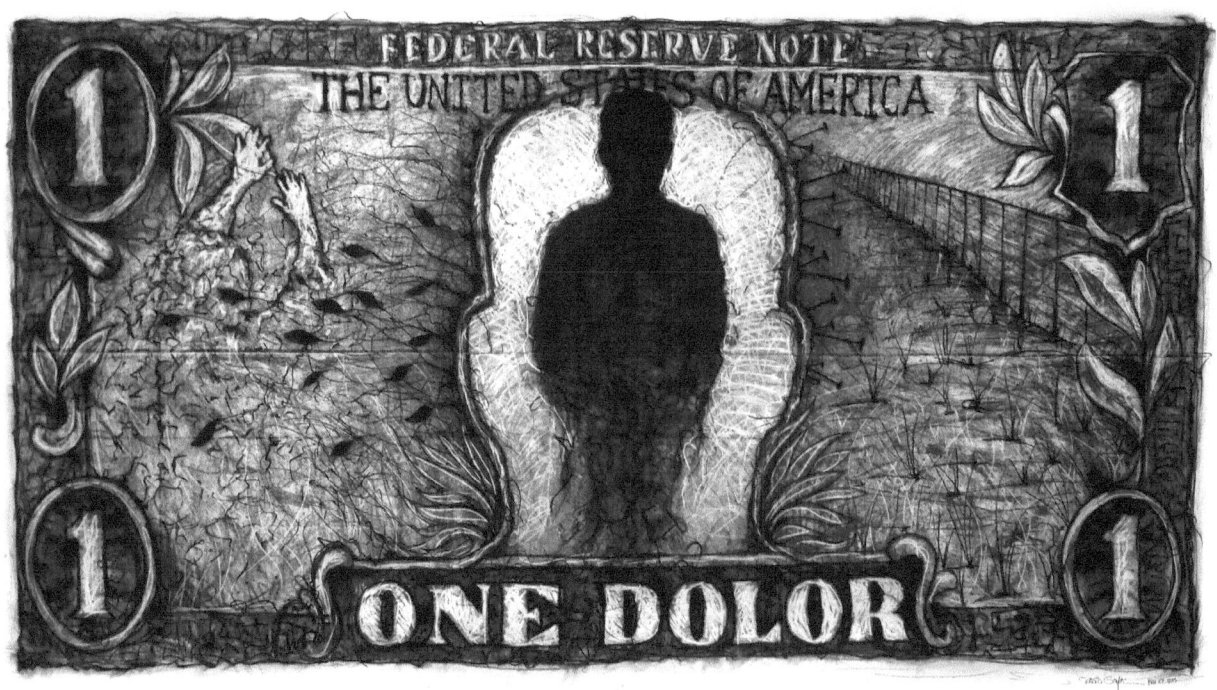

One Dolor/One Pain
Medium: charcoal on paper
Size: 100 x 176 in

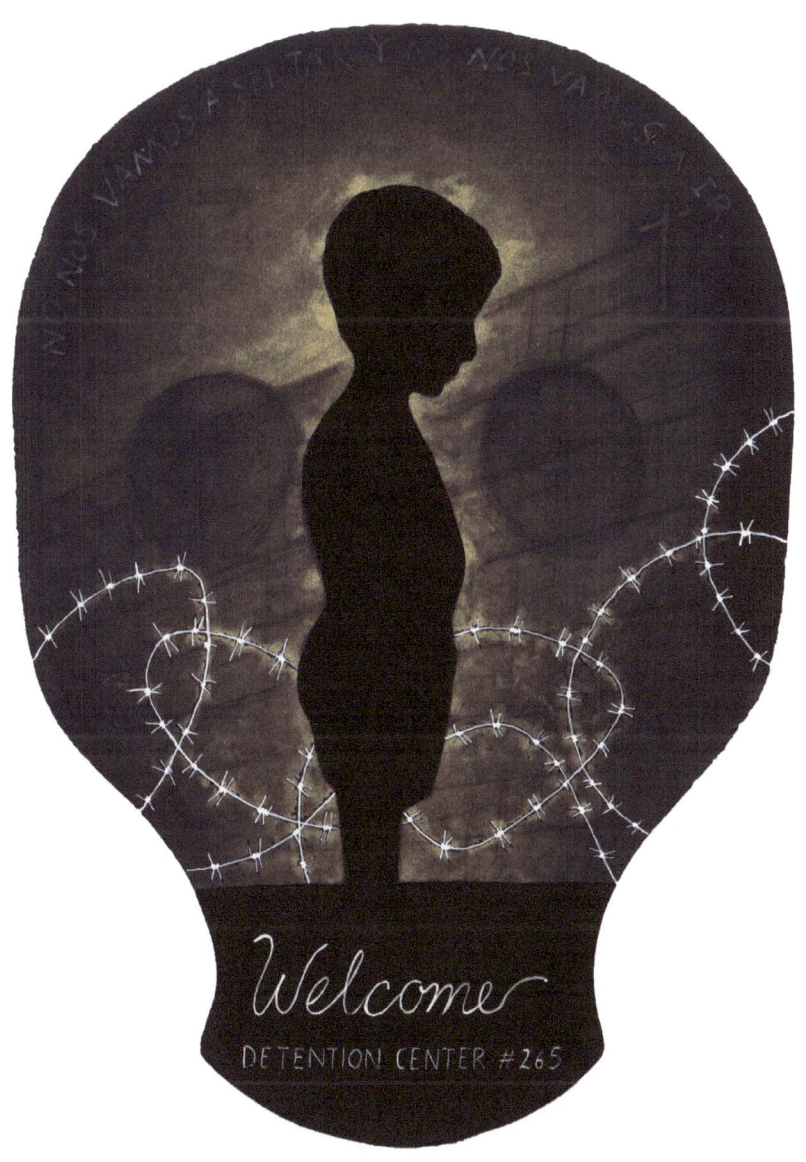

Welcome to Detention Center #265
Medium: Acrylic and charcoal on wood
Size: 18 x 24 in

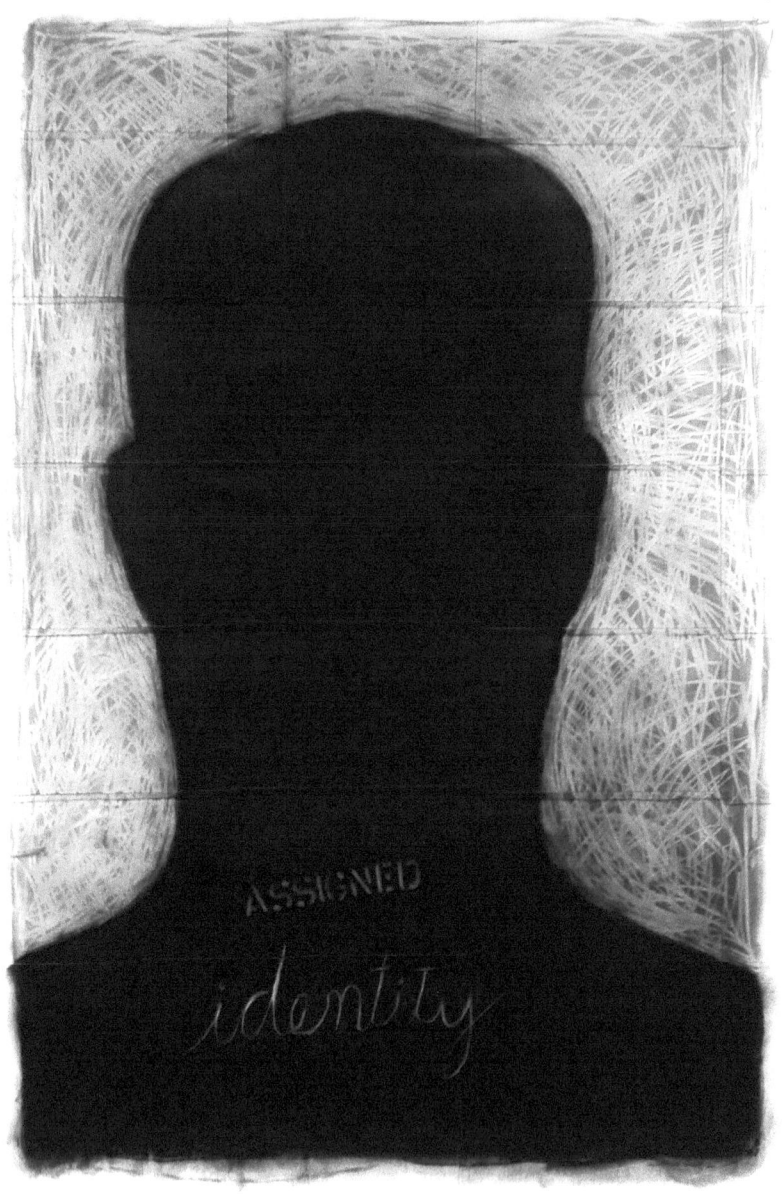

Assigned Identity
Inventory Number: 038
Medium: Charcoal on Paper/Canvas

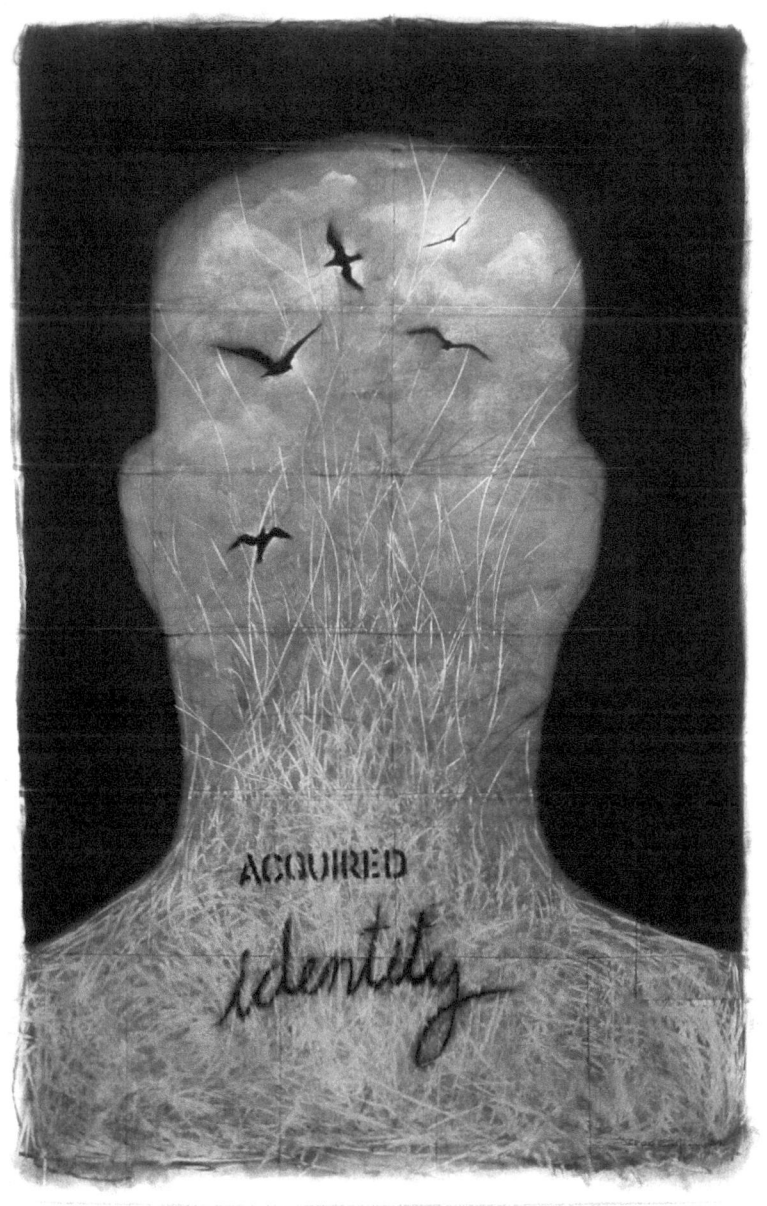

Acquired Identity
Medium: Charcoal on Paper/Canvas
Size: 90 x 50 in

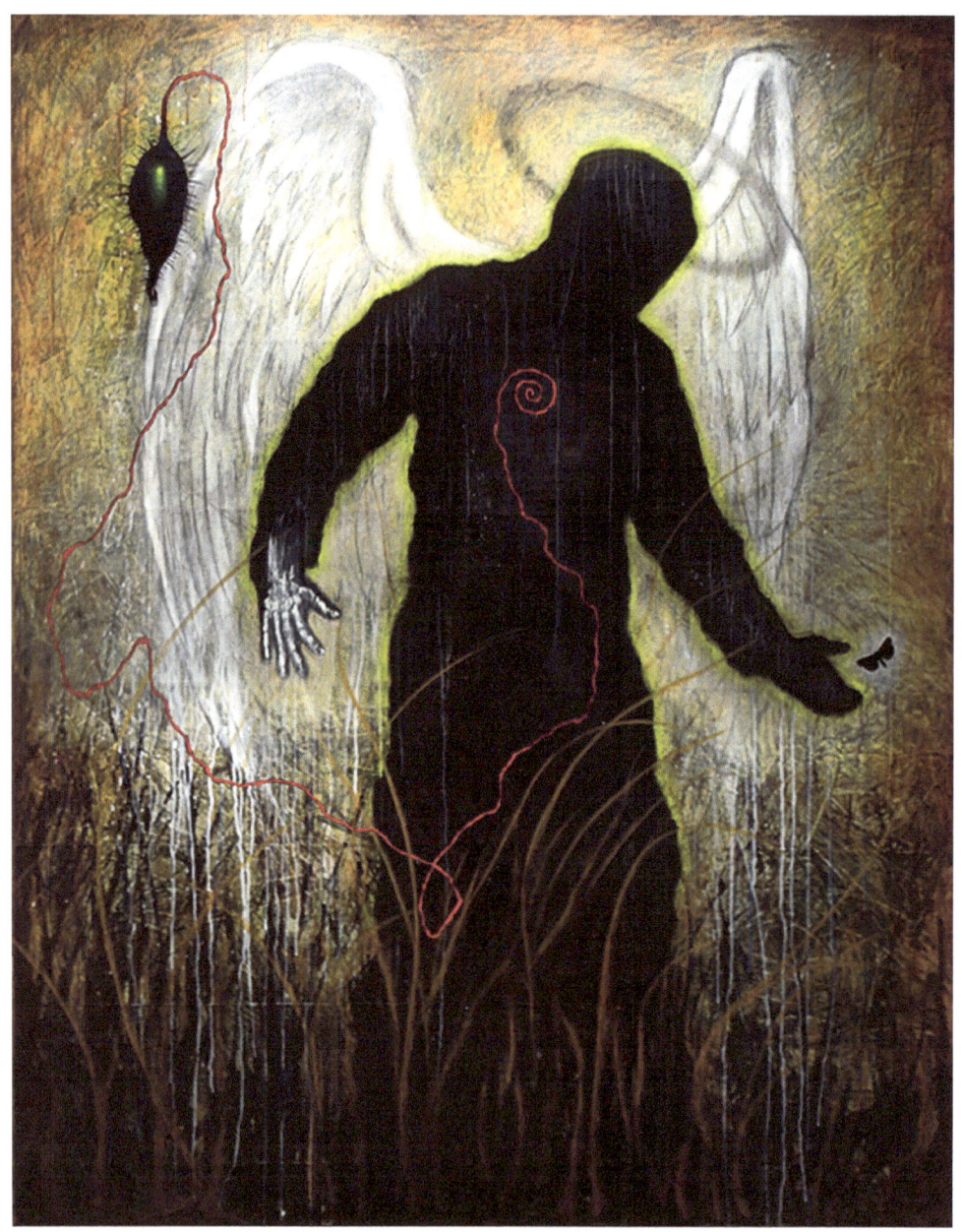

Death of Paradise
Medium: Acrylic On Canvas
Size: 72 x 82 in

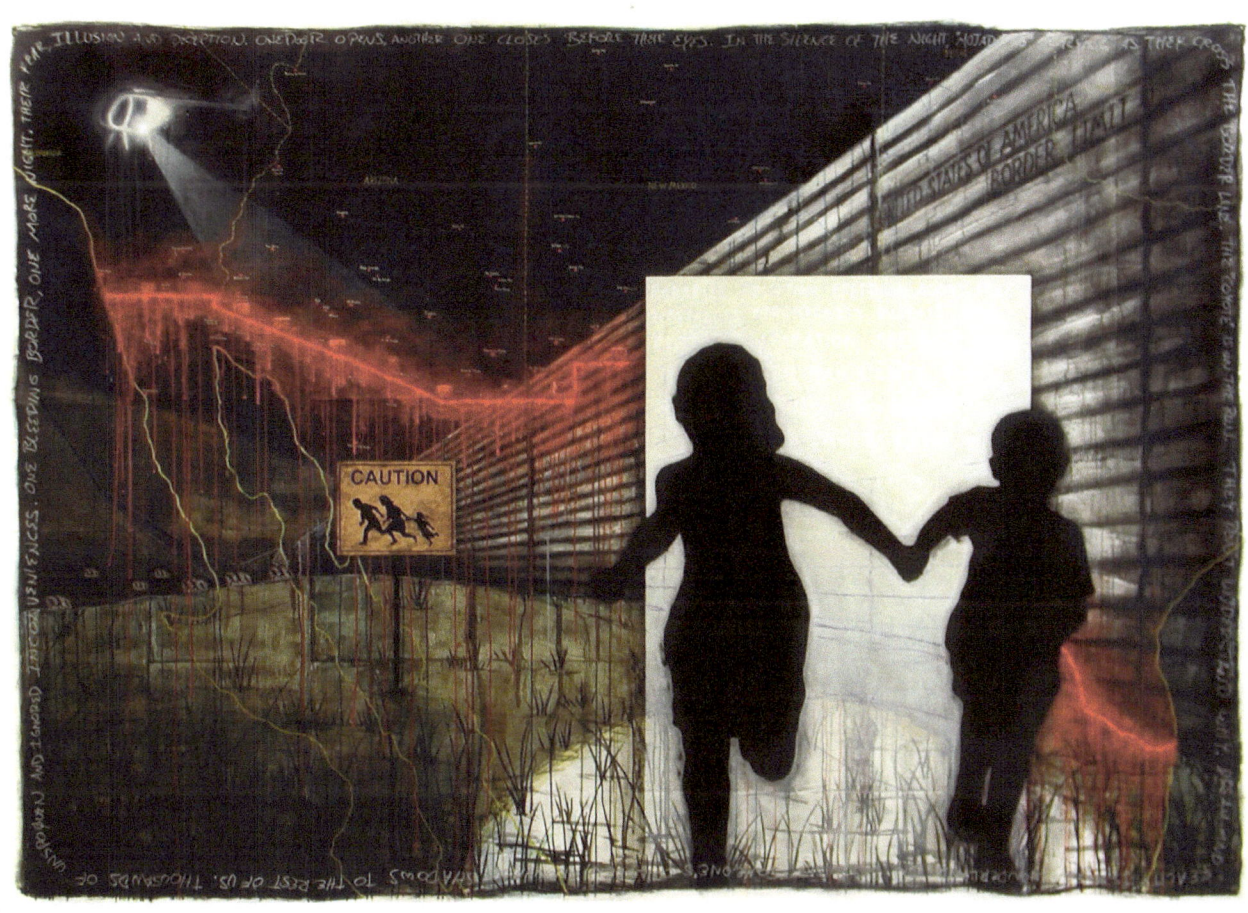

The Bleeding Border
Medium: Acrylic on Paper/Canvas
Size: 77 x 112 in

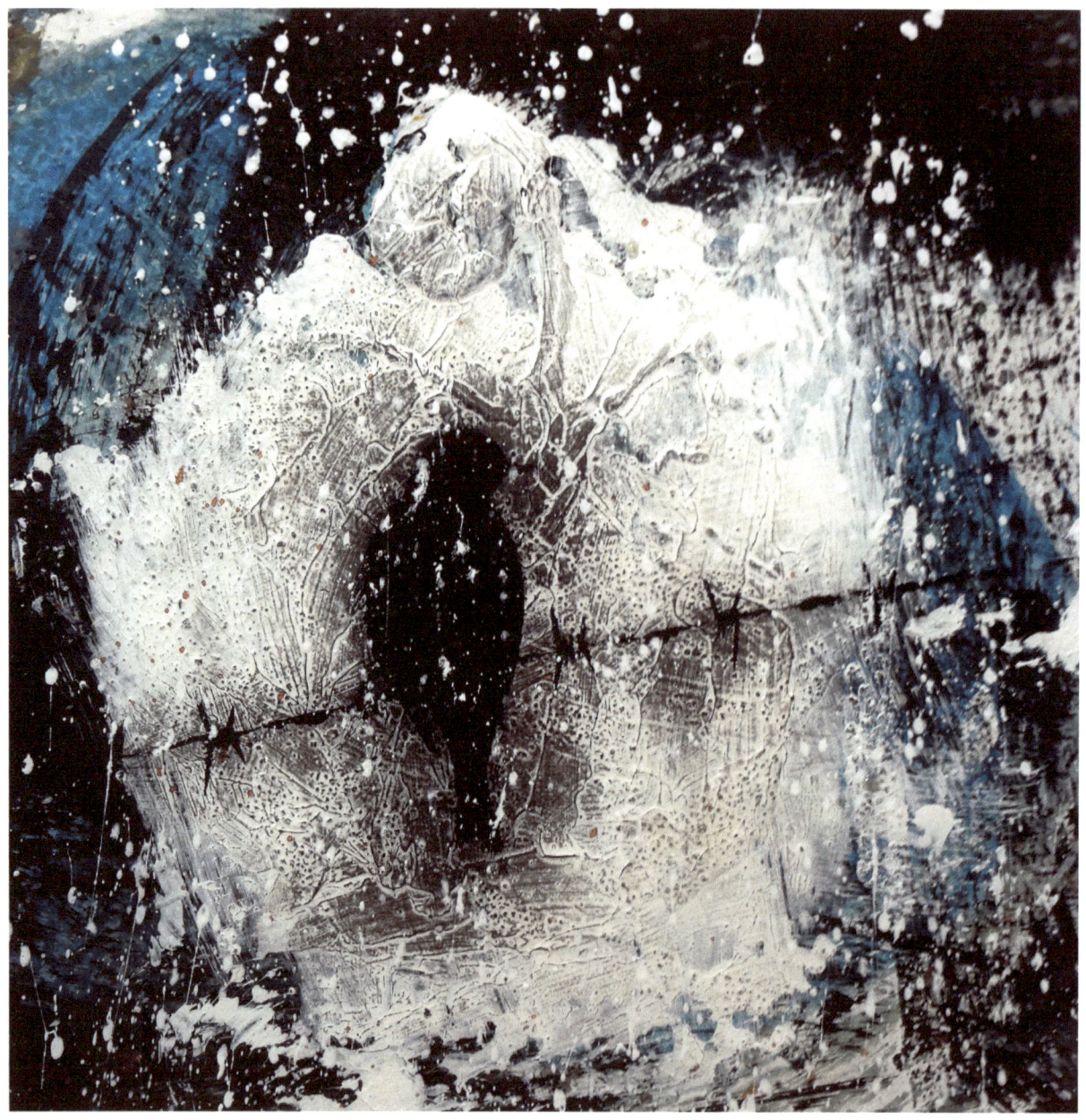

Winter Wait 1
Medium: Acrylic on wood
Size: 12 x 12 x 2 in

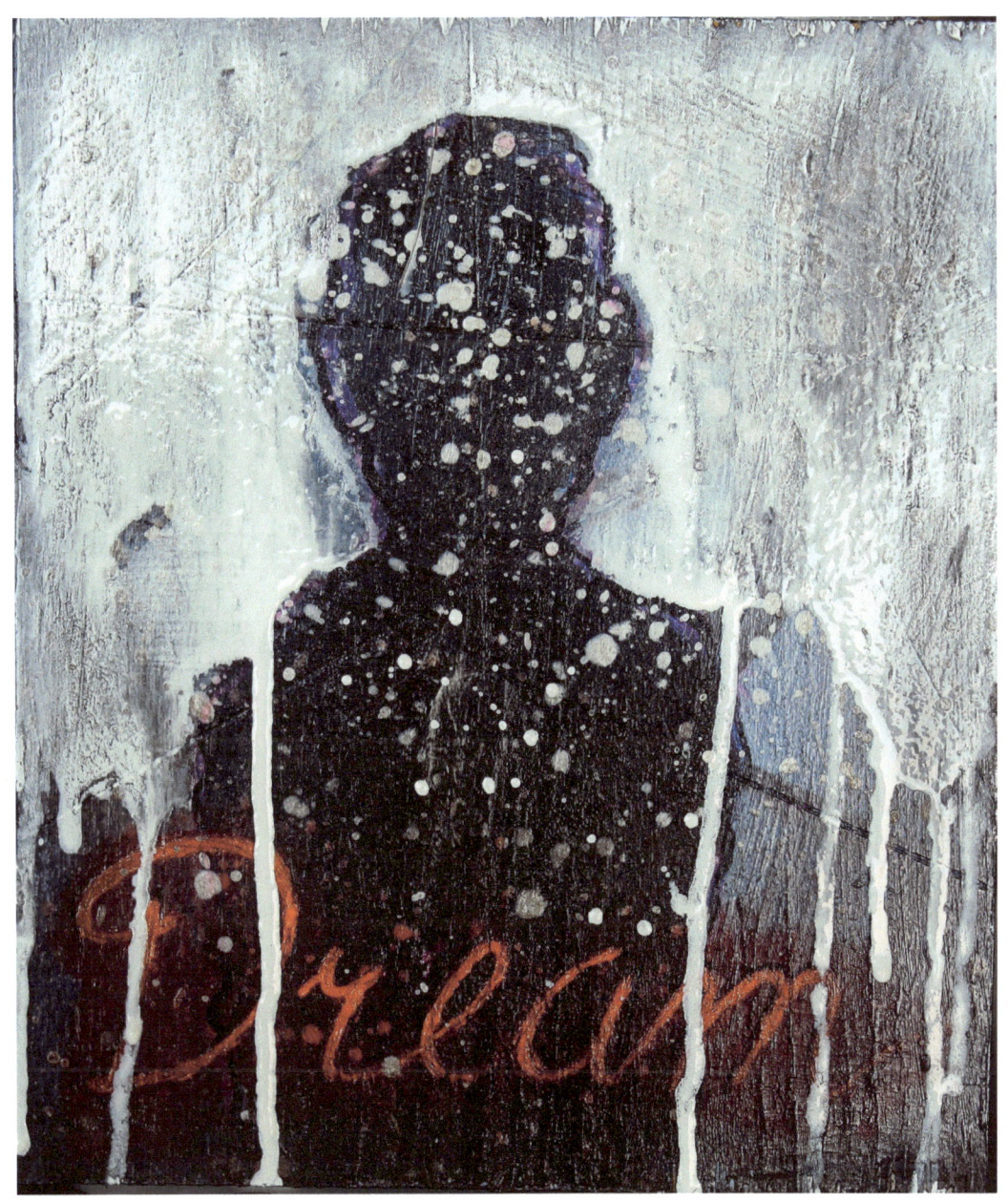

The Immigrant's Way: Dream
Medium: Acrylic on Wood
Size: 8 x 7 in

The Immigrant's Way: Love
Medium: Acrylic on Wood

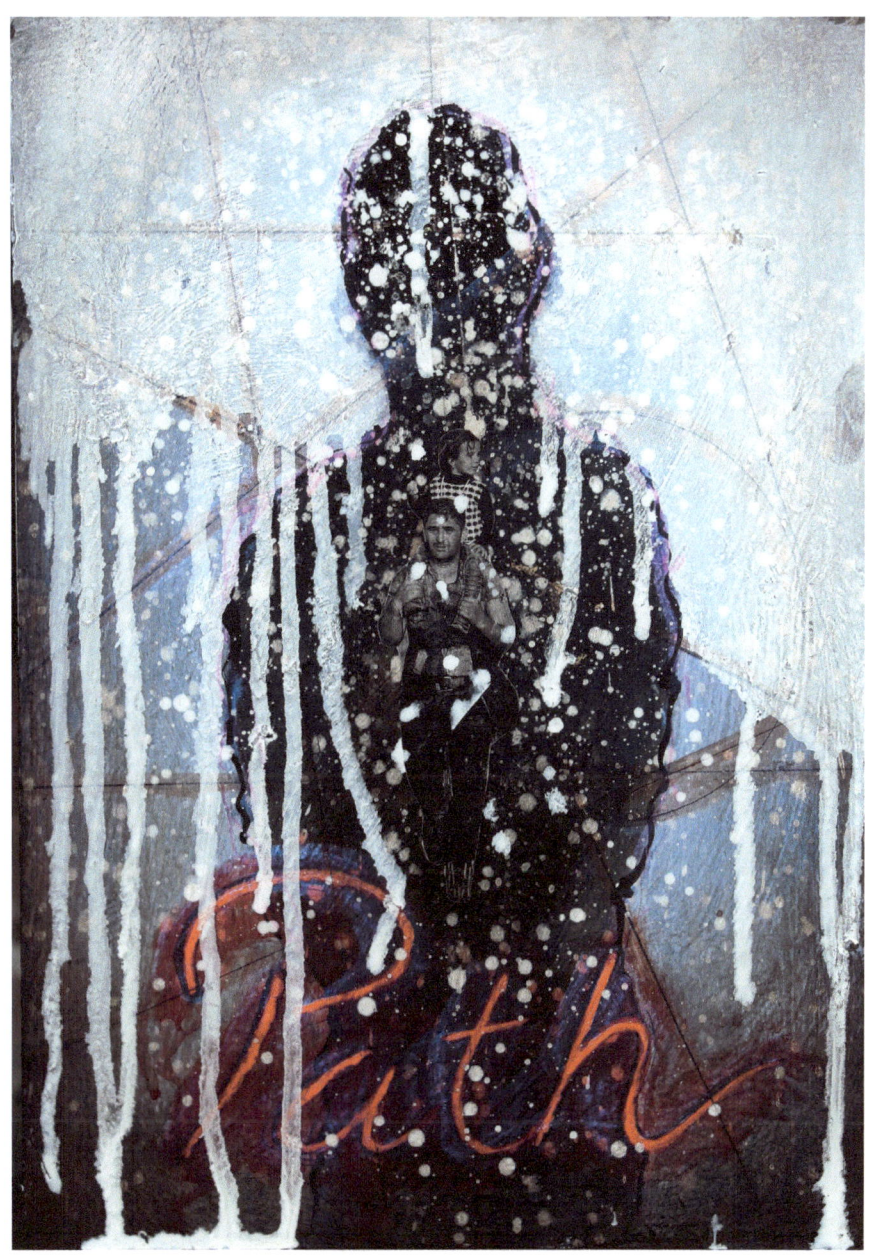

The Immigrant's Way: Path
Medium: Acrylic on Wood
Size: 13 x 9 in

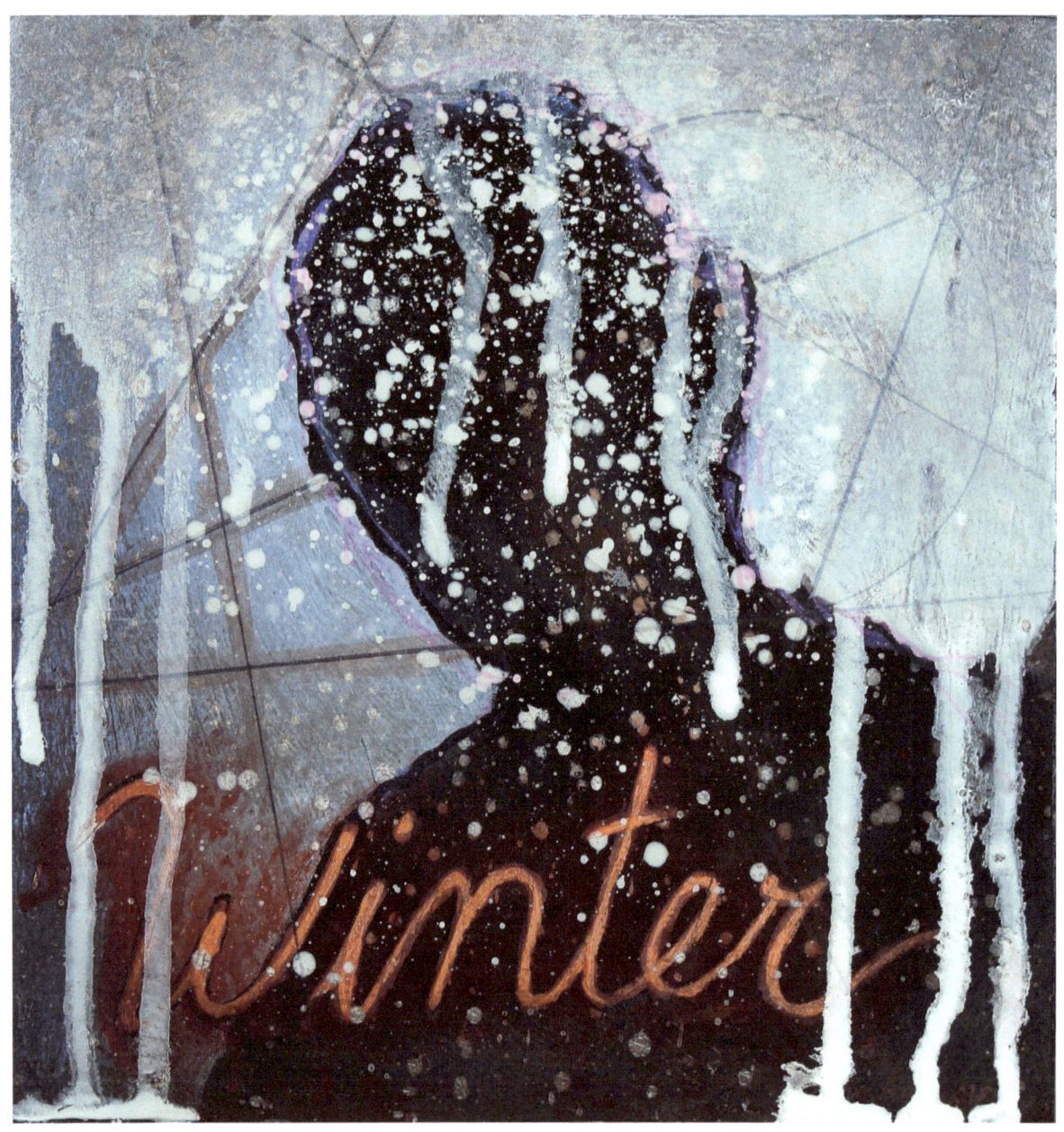

The Immigrant's Way: Winter
Medium: Acrylic on Wood
Size: 8 x 8 x 2 in

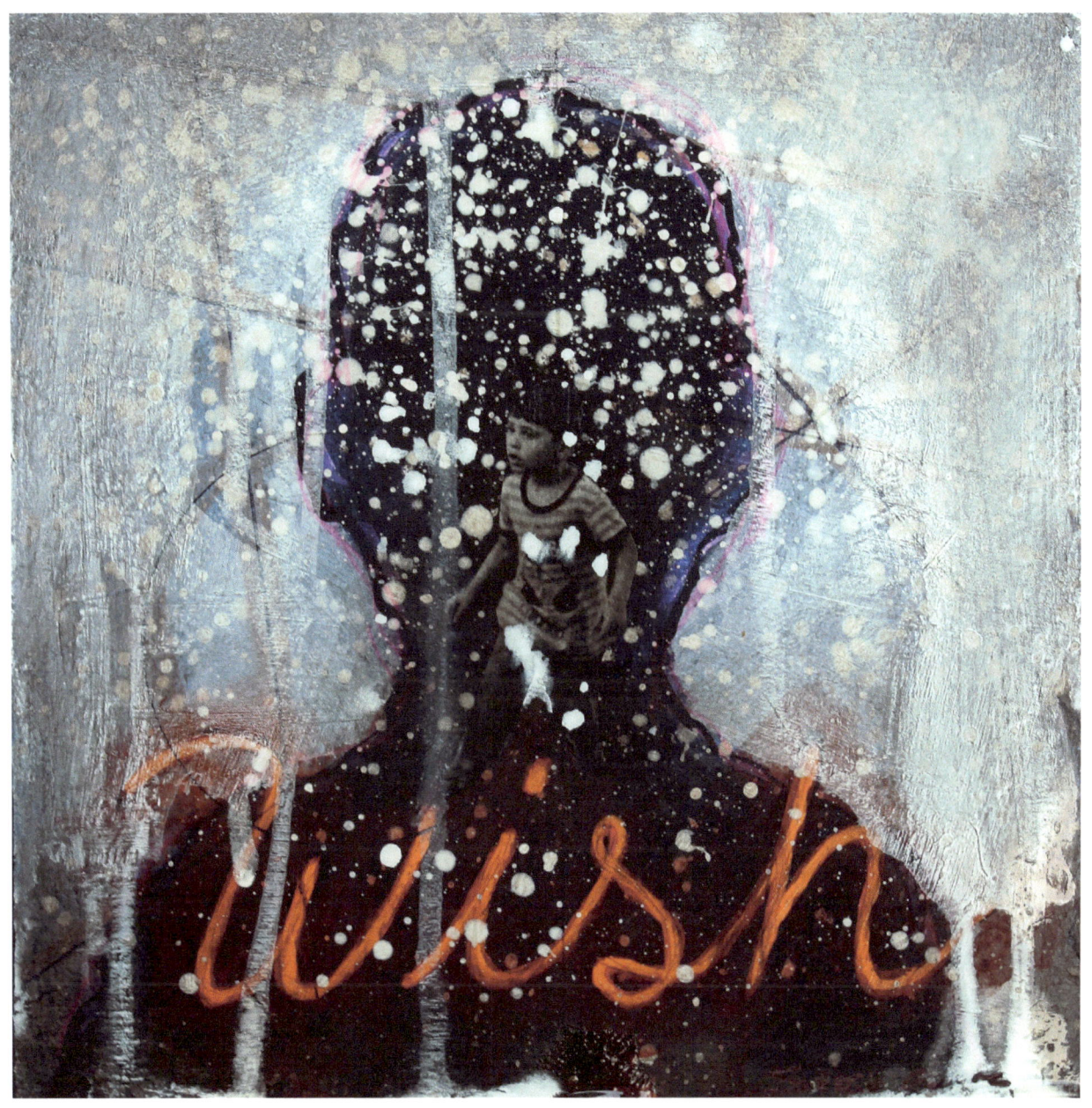

The Immigrant's Way: Wish
Medium: Acrylic on Wood
Size: 8 x 8 x 2 in

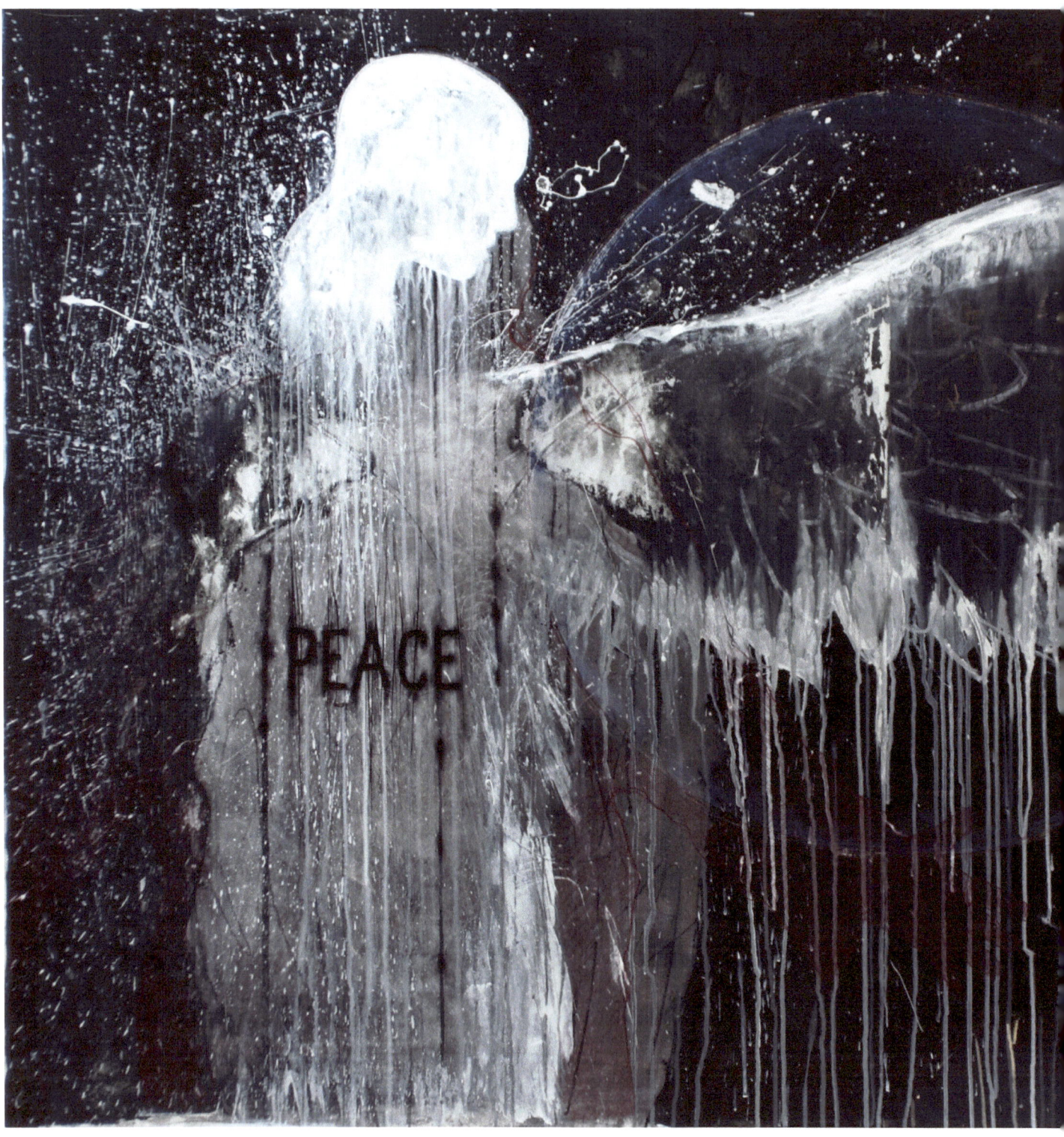

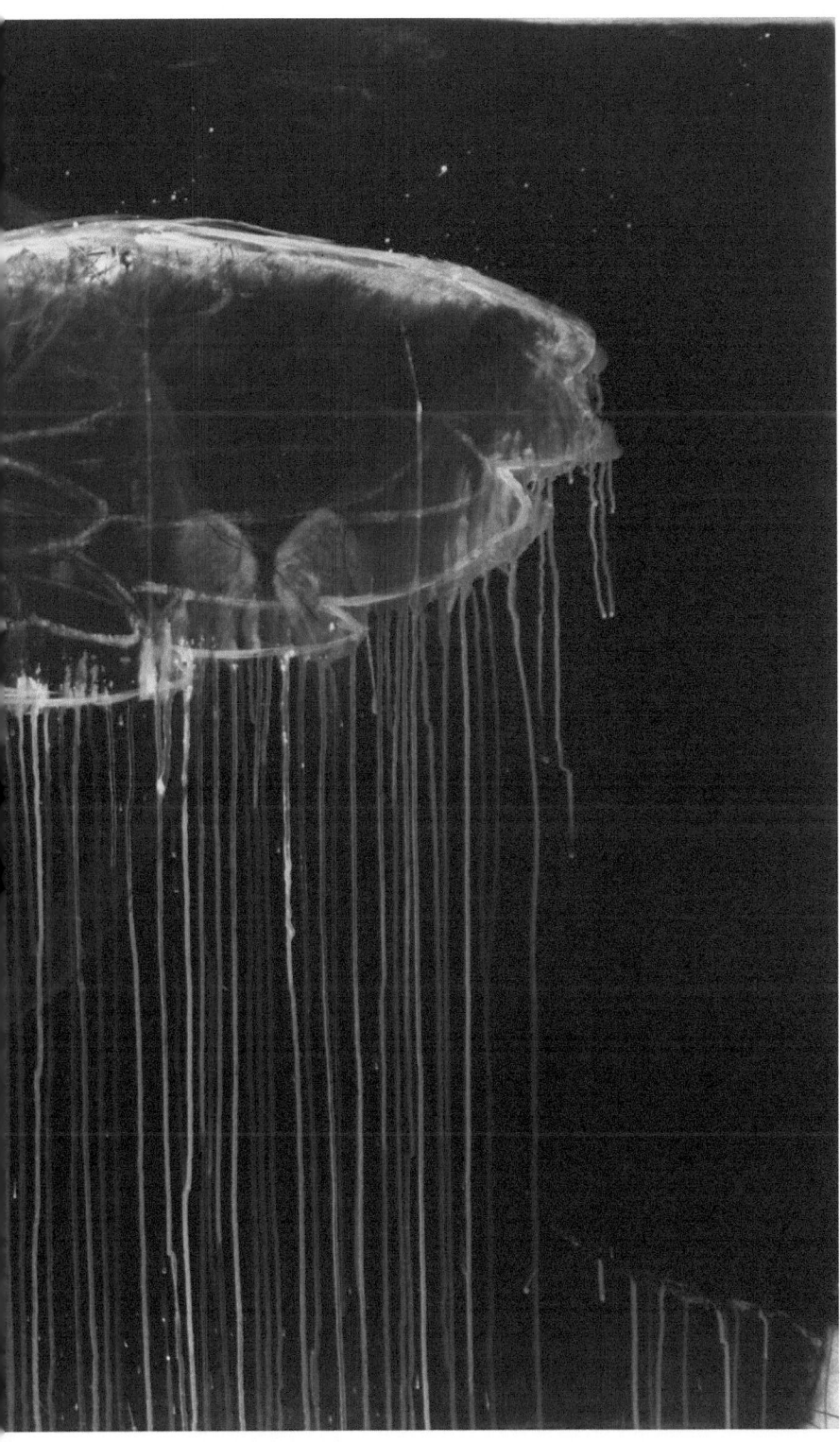

Spirit of Peace
Medium: Acrylic and charcoal on paper / canvas
Size: 42 x 56 in

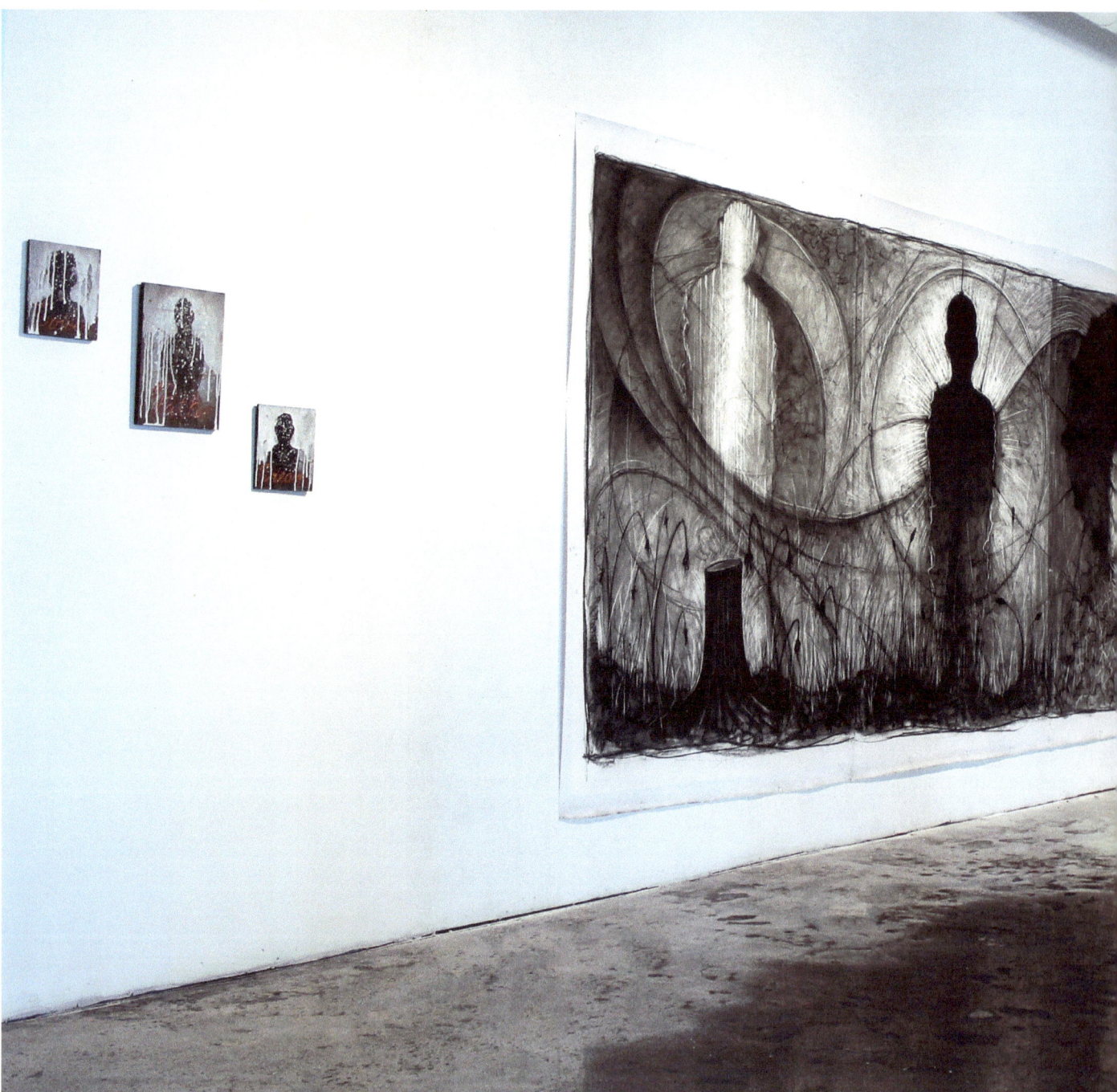

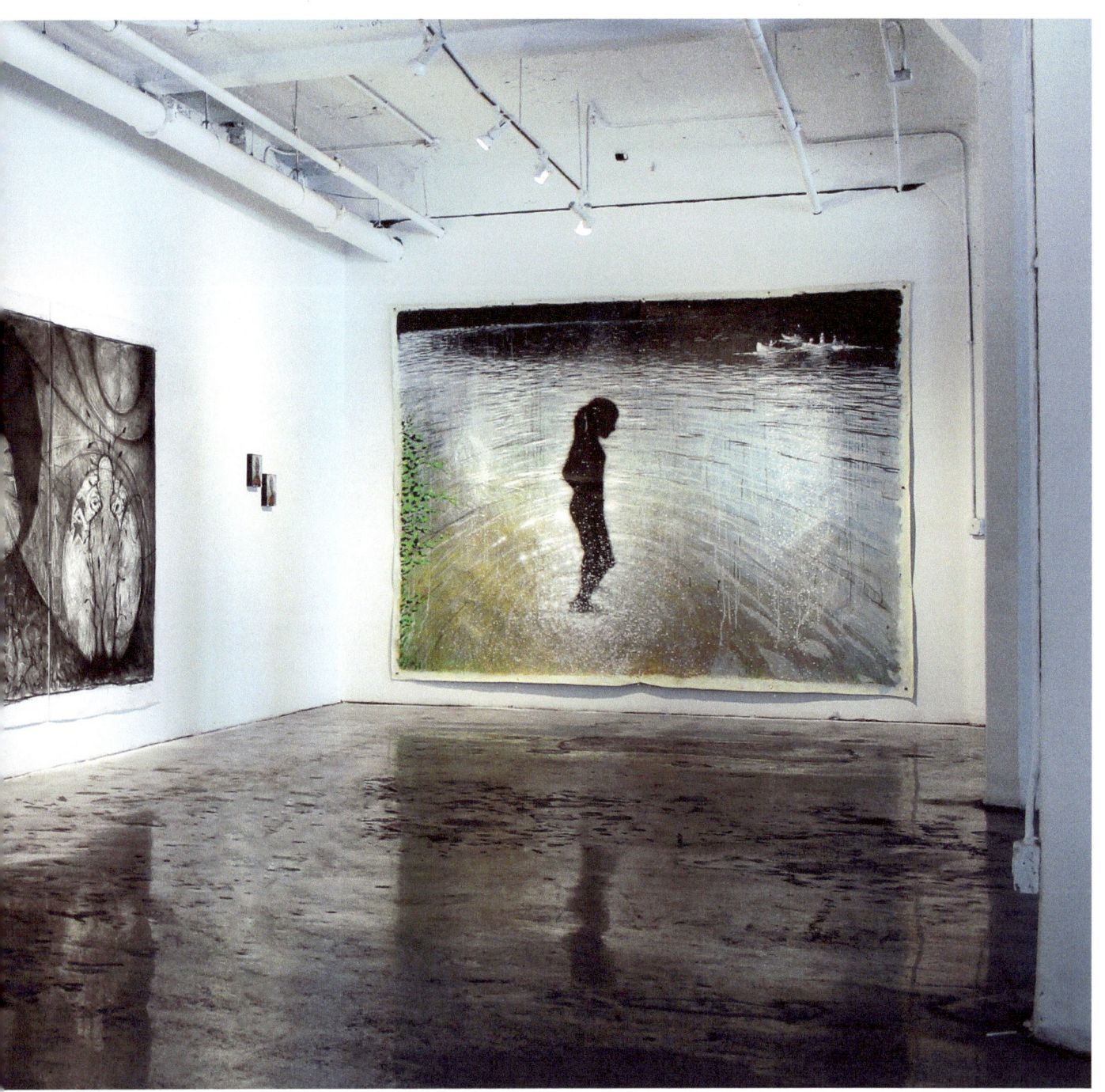

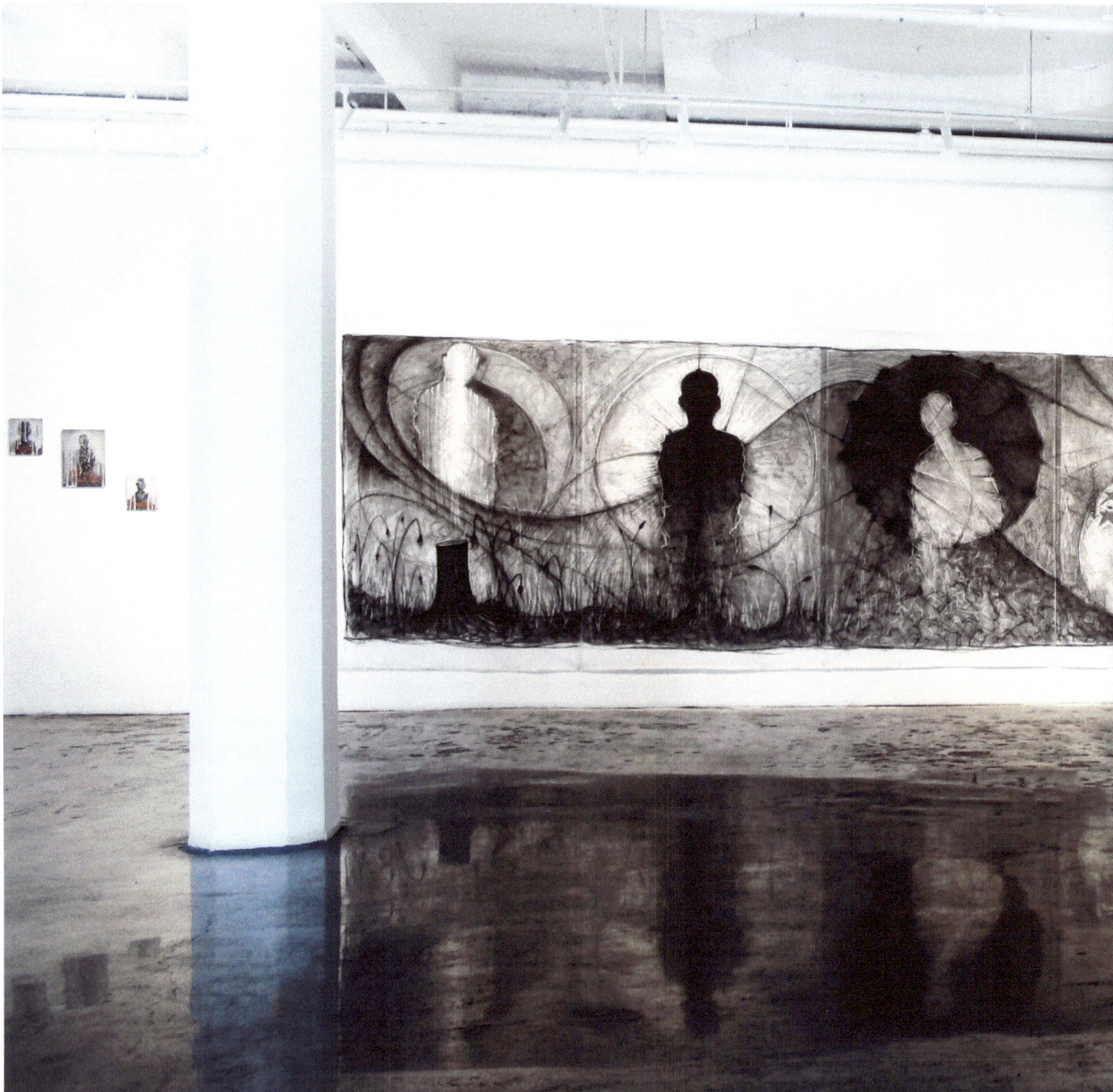

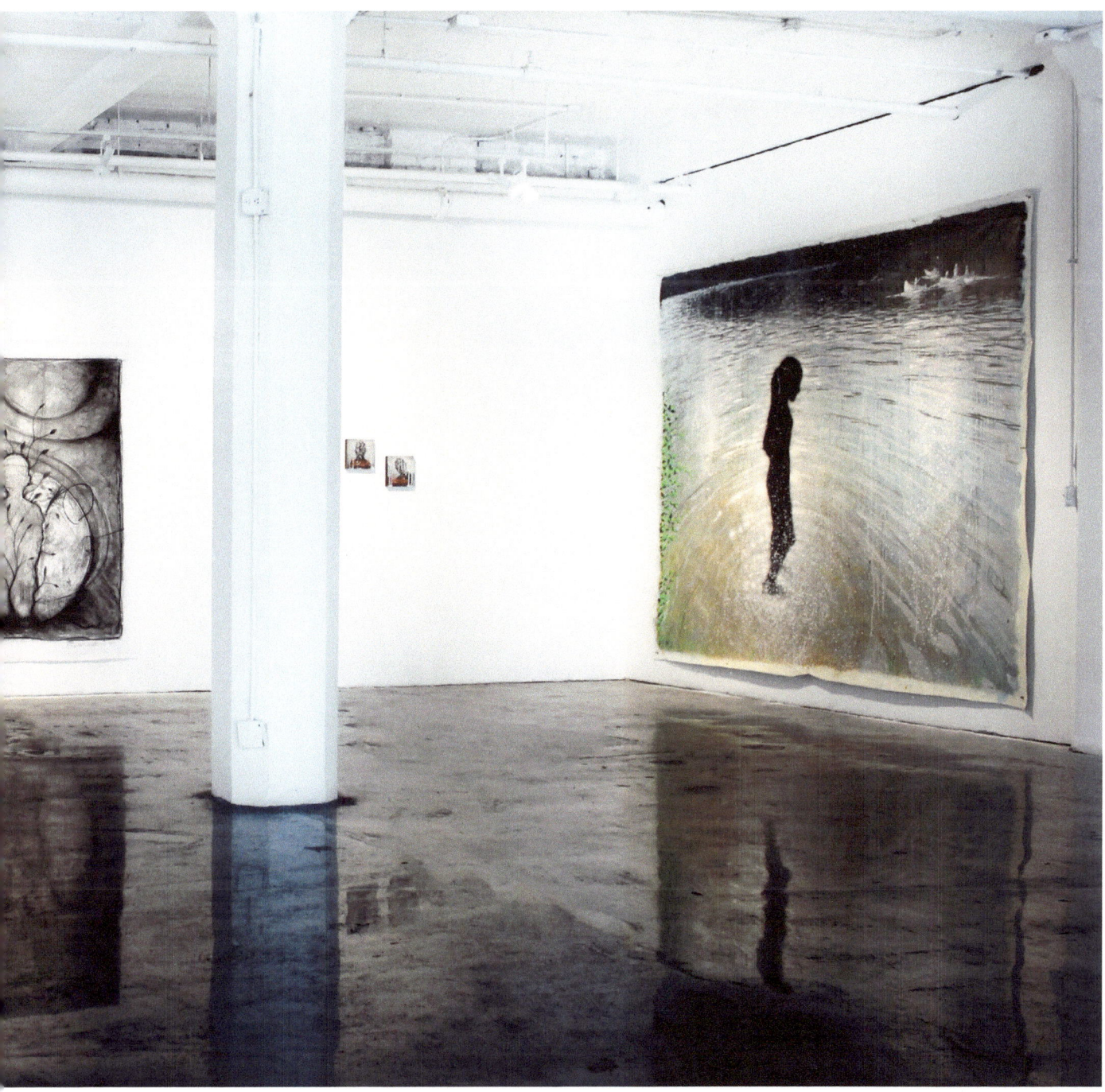

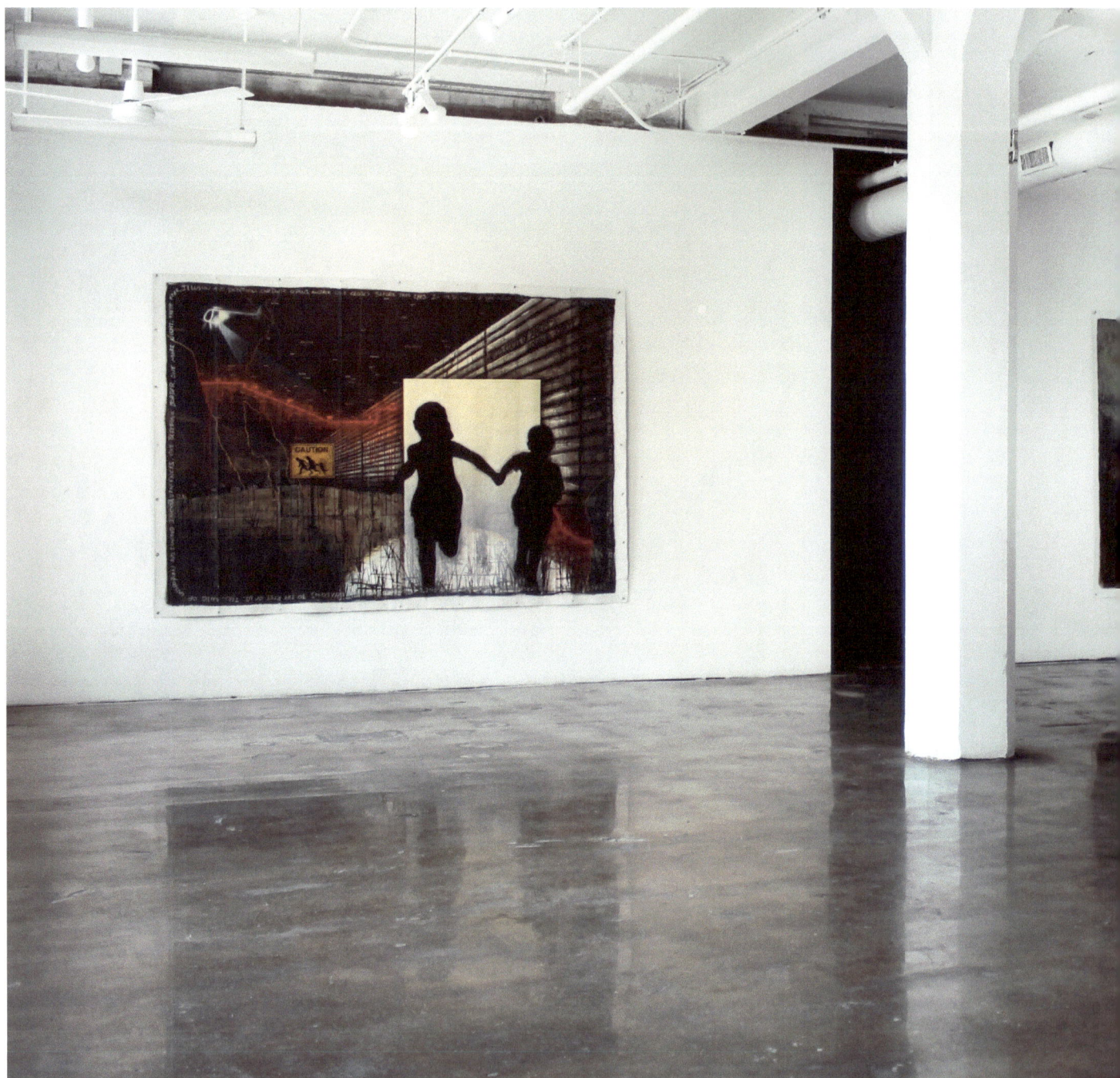

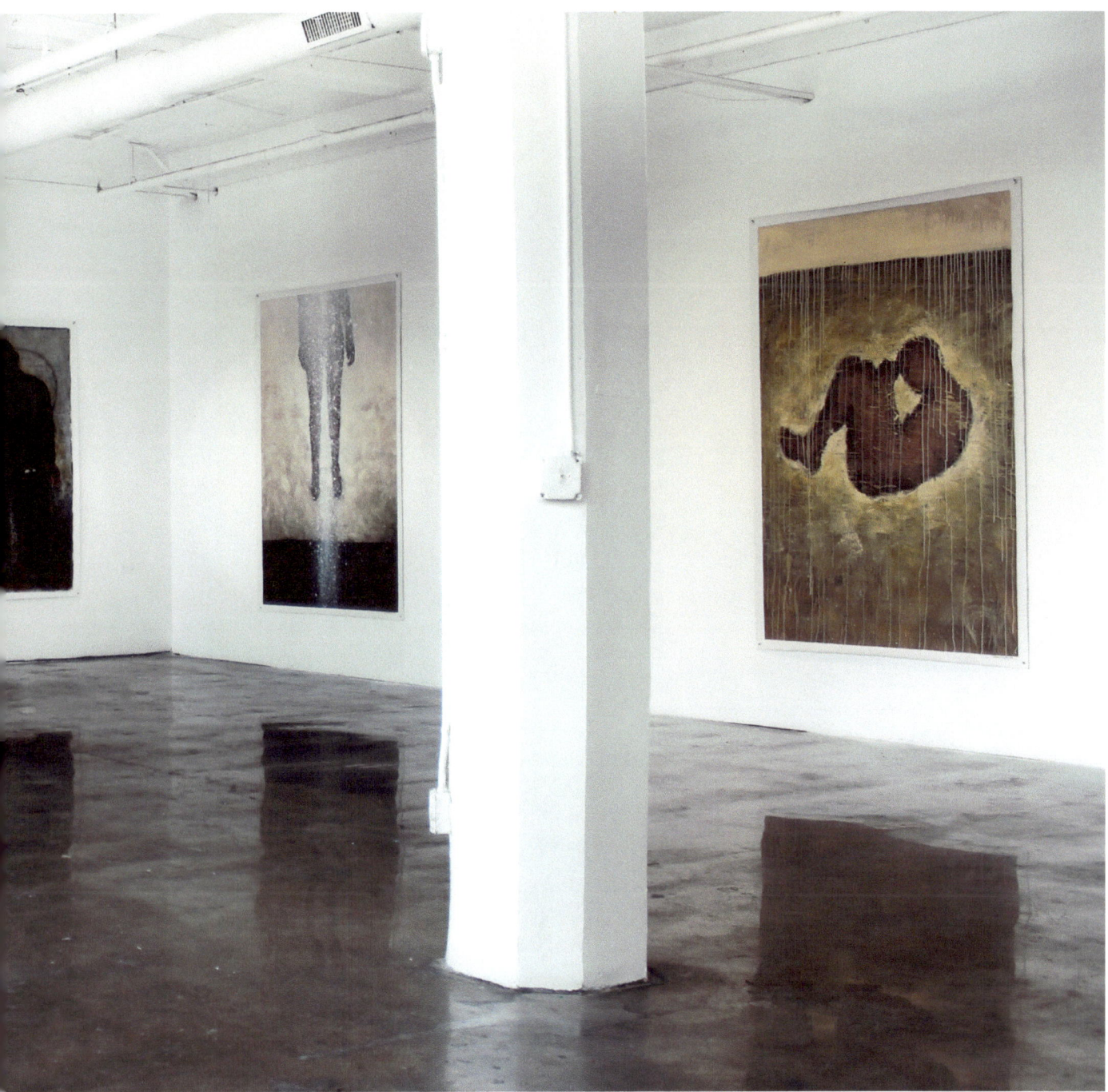

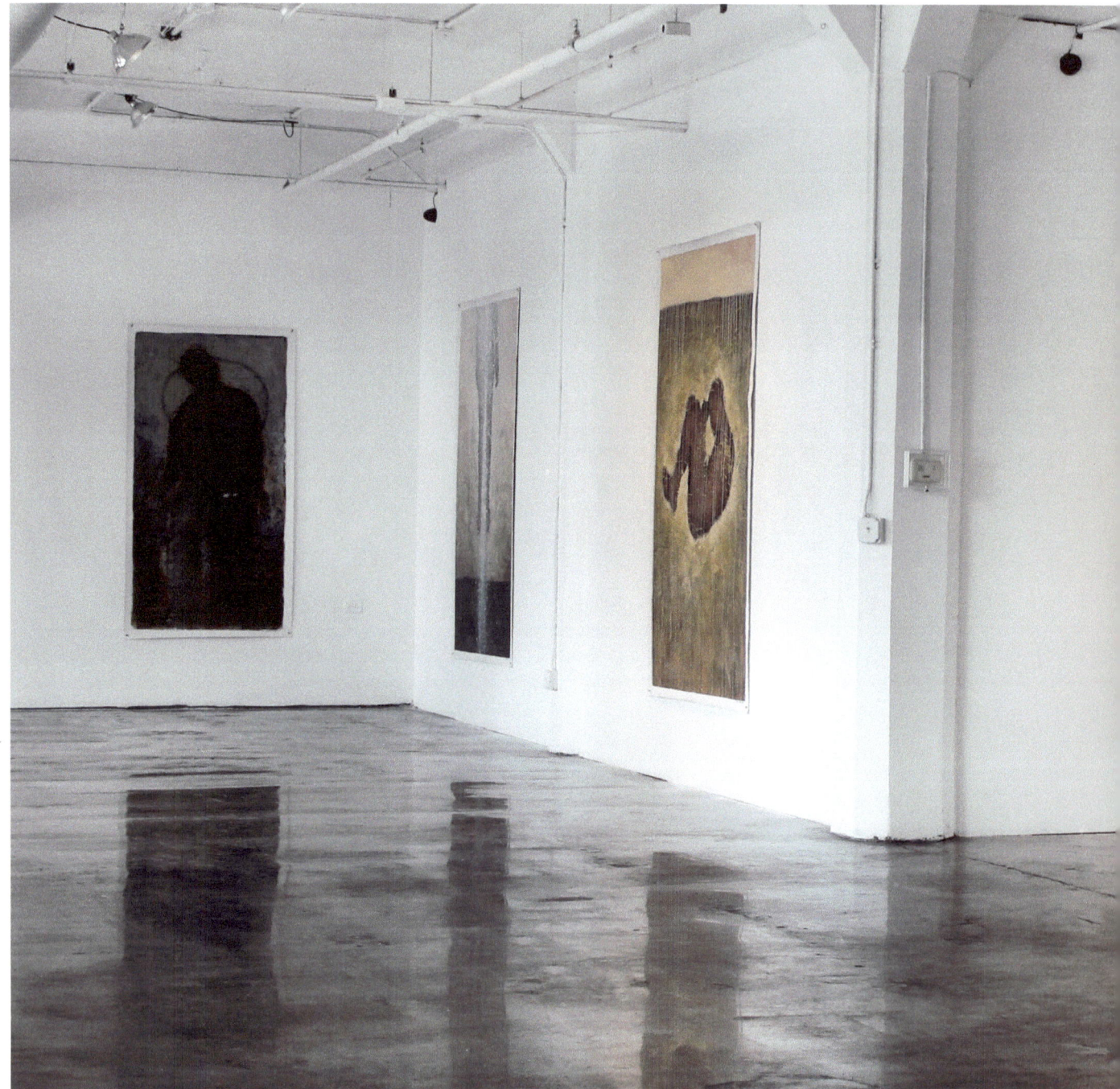

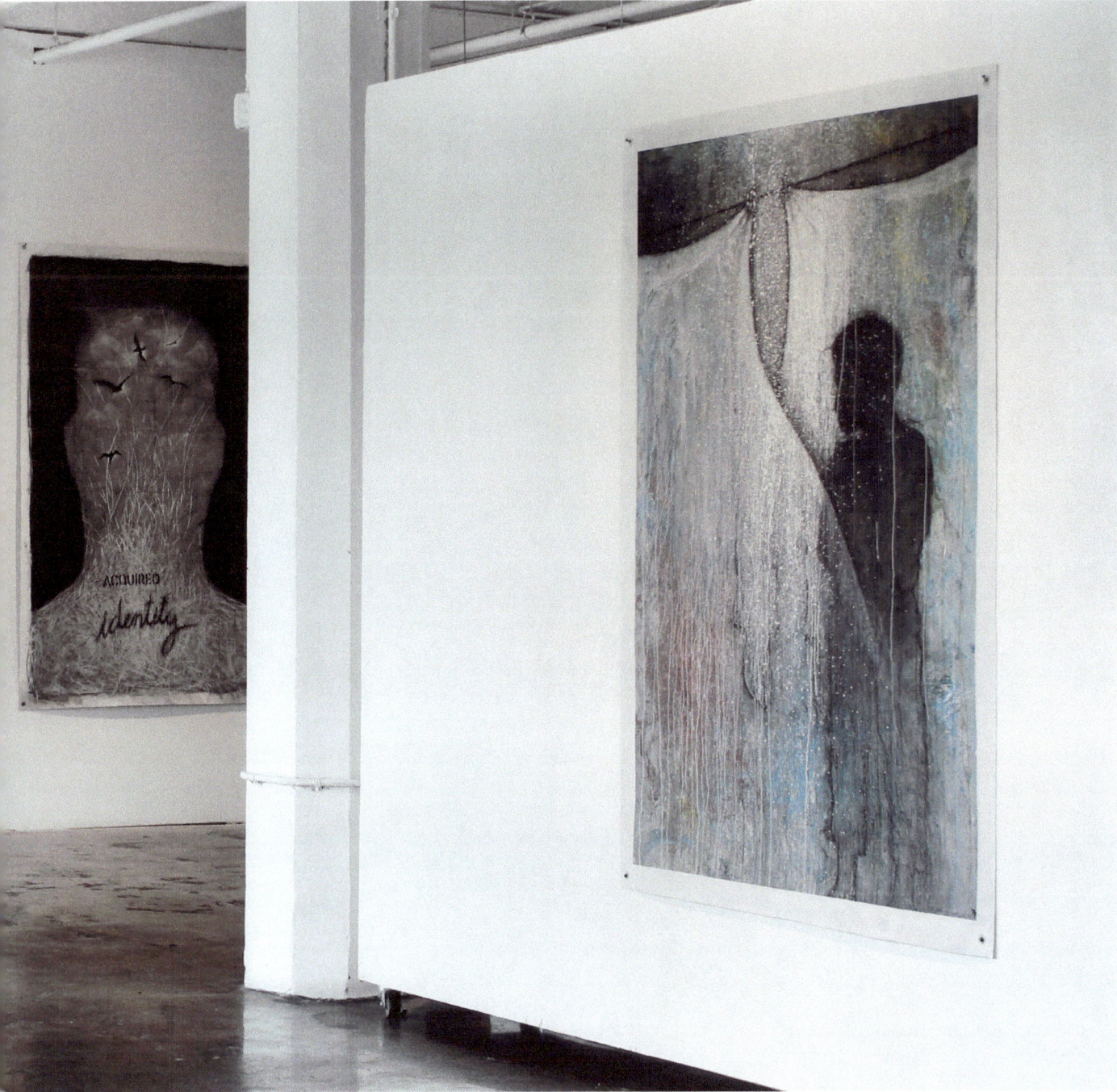

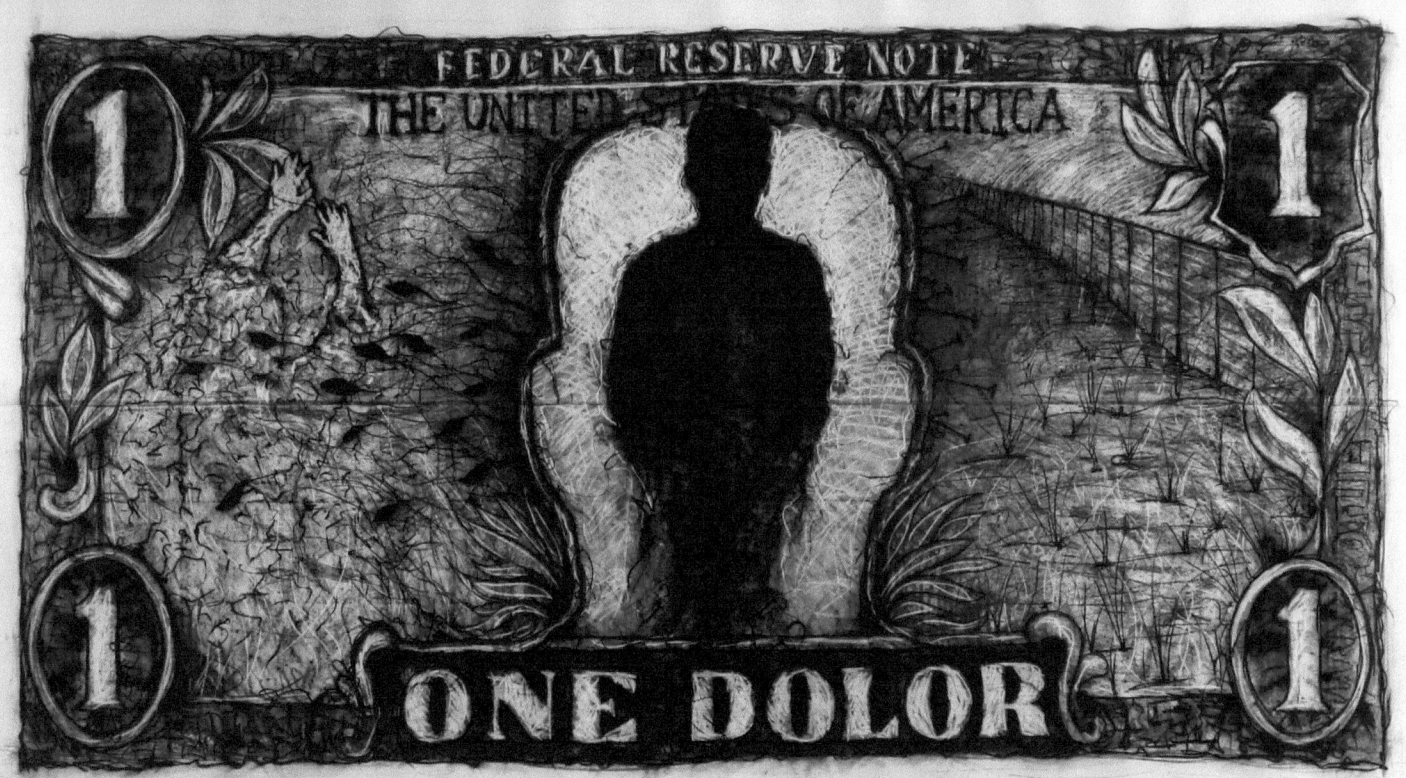